THE KANSAS CITY ST

NUMBER 5

◆

George Brett and
The Kansas City Royals

Andrews and McMeel
A Universal Press Syndicate Company
Kansas City

NUMBER 5

George Brett and The Kansas City Royals

Editor:
David A. Zeeck

Text editors:
Dale Bye
Dale Phelps

Photo editor:
Dan Peak

Contributing photographers:
Fred Blocher, Joe Coleman, Steve
Gonzales, Joe Ledford, Tammy Ljungblad,
Jim McTaggart, Keith Myers, Dan Seifert,
John Sleezer, Rick Solberg, John Spink.

Contributing writers:
Jo-Ann Barnas, Del Black, Dale Bye,
Sid Bordman, Steve Cameron, Mike
DeArmond, Dennis Dodd, Jack Etkin,
Mike Fish, Jeffrey Flanagan, Dick Kaegel,
Joe McGuff, Mike McKenzie, Bob
Nightengale, Dale Phelps, Tracy Ringolsby,
Gib Twyman.

Special acknowledgments:
Dale Phelps, for his encyclopedic
knowledge and his personal library of
Royals lore; Jim McTaggart, for his contri-
bution to overall photo selection; Dale Bye,
Steve Paul, Patricia Person and Rosanne
Wickman, title suggestions; and Jack
Stevenson, George Brett's baseball coach at
El Segundo High School.

Front cover photo:
Joe Ledford

Back cover photo:
Cliff Schiappa, AP

Cover and Book Design:
Travis Williams,
Output Technologies, Design Group

Andrews and McMeel

Managing Editor:
Dorothy O'Brien

Production:
Carol Coe, Cathy Kirkland

Pre-Press:
Chromagraphics

Printing:
Clark Printing, Liberty, Missouri

THE KANSAS CITY STAR.

Publisher:
Bob Woodworth

Editor:
Arthur S. Brisbane

Managing Editors:
Jane Amari
Mark Zieman

Library of Congress Catalog Card Number: 93-74101

ISBN: 0-8362-8055-5

First Printing, November 1993
Third Printing, March 1994

CONTENTS

◆

♦ George Brett's intensity made him one of baseball's all-time great hitters. (1985 photo)

FOREWORD

◆

By JOE McGUFF

Joe McGuff worked at The Kansas City Star *from 1948 to 1992 as a sportswriter, columnist, sports editor and editor. He was the beat reporter on the Kansas City Athletics for 11 years and covered the Royals as a columnist. He was inducted into the writer's wing of the Baseball Hall of Fame in 1985.*

It was the morning after George Brett's final game at Kauffman Stadium. A young father was talking about the emotional impact of the occasion and how glad he was that he took his 5-year-old son.

"He probably won't remember it," he said, "but I wanted him to be able to say he saw George Brett play."

The Hall of Fame is the vehicle that baseball uses to recognize its greatest players. But the public has its own way of recognizing greatness, and for the most part its standards are even more demanding.

Baseball fans talk almost reverentially of having seen a Babe Ruth, a Stan Musial, a Ted Williams, a Hank Aaron. It is a measure of George Brett's greatness that he is in this class.

Brett is the only player in major-league history with at least 3,000 hits, 600 doubles, 100 triples, 300 homers and 200 stolen bases. He is the only player to win batting titles in three decades (1976, 1980 and 1990). He is 11th on baseball's all-time list in hits with 3,154, 10th in extra-base hits with 1,119, fifth in doubles with 665, 18th in total bases with 5,044, and tied for 22nd in runs batted in with 1,595.

Although statistics offer a convenient way to measure the comparative talents of players, Brett's greatness transcends mere numbers. He played 21 seasons with the Royals in an era when players have become mercenaries who auction themselves off to the highest bidder. Brett's name was synonymous with his team. He carried the image in Kansas City that Musial did in St. Louis, that Williams did in Boston and that Willie Mays did with the Giants.

Legally the Royals were Ewing Kauffman's team, but in the eyes of their fans they were George Brett's team.

Unlike a Mays or a Williams or a Mickey Mantle, Brett did not come to the majors with awesome statistics. Even so, when Brett came to spring training with the Royals in 1974, scouts from other organizations rated him as "can't miss."

But, in looking back on the spring of '74, it is safe to say that no one, myself included, was writing about the possibility of Brett becoming a superstar.

The first person to talk about Brett in those terms was the late Charley Lau, the Royals hitting coach. Lau taught the importance of hitters using the entire field, and in Brett he found the perfect pupil. Whitey Herzog, who became the Royals manager late in the 1975 season, also predicted a great future for Brett, but he and Lau were at odds because Herzog liked Brett's power and thought he should look for more balls to pull.

My early recollections of Brett are not so much those of a budding superstar but of someone who ran out every ball, broke up double plays, chewed tobacco, stayed out late, got to the park early and was a throwback to an earlier era. He loved life, and he loved baseball.

What no one could foresee, including Lau and Herzog, was that extraordinary quality in Brett's makeup that enabled him to play at an almost superhuman level in big games. I can say without reservation that George Brett is the greatest clutch player I have ever seen.

In years to come, Brett probably will be best remembered for his home run against the Yankees' Goose Gossage that sent the Royals into the 1980 World Series. But to me the performance that stands out above the rest came in the third game of the 1985 American League Championship Series with Toronto.

The Royals lost the first two games in Toronto, stretching their streak of post-season losses to 10. The Royals took a plane home from Toronto, but a hearse would have been a more suitable conveyance.

At this juncture it seemed that only Superman could save the Royals. And Superman did. Never has one player so dominated a crucial game. Brett homered in the first inning. In the third he made a brilliant backhanded stop behind third base and threw out a runner trying to score from third. He hit a double two feet from the top of the left-field wall in the fourth. In the sixth he homered to deep left-center. To complete his resuscitation of the Royals, he singled in the eighth and scored the winning run in a 6-5 victory.

Once Brett established himself in the majors, he was confident of his ability, but I sometimes wondered whether he ever realized just how good he was. One year in spring training I asked him whether he had ever set a goal of becoming the best hitter in baseball. He looked at me as if the thought had never entered his mind. Then he shook his head, made a few remarks about hitting and said, "It's so hard."

It is difficult for us to accept that we will never again see No. 5 hitting a game-winning home run, driving an outside pitch to left field, charging down the line on a two-hopper to second or breaking up a double play. When George left the ballpark for the last time, all of us walked with him. It was a day we all felt a little older and a little sad.

Now all we have are the memories, and that is the reason for this book. They are wonderful memories, and from time to time it will lift our spirits to revisit a career that made our lives a little more exciting and sometimes filled us with awe. ◆

BRETT ACCEPTED CHALLENGE OF GREATNESS

◆

By JACK ETKIN

October 2, 1992

The outs are strewn along the roadside, thousands and thousands of them after so many years. Countless pop-ups, innumerable line drives and a legion of lazy flies have sailed to every reach of the field.

More infinite still are the ground balls. On his way to 3,000 hits, George Brett hit one-hoppers, high-hoppers and short-hoppers as well as no-hoppers that trickled through the infield grass or hugged the artificial turf.

Brett's rhythmic left-handed swing has made the second baseman the most frequent target of these grounders. With every one, at the moment of contact, Brett begins a 90-foot dash. Again.

His chances of beating the second baseman's throw are as slim as the doomed Sisyphus in Hades. Time after time, the greedy king pushed a heavy stone toward the top of the hill, only to have it roll down again. Time after time, Brett has taken off at full speed, conceding nothing.

"Sometimes it's like a game," Brett said. "I want to see how close I can come to being safe. You know you're not going to be safe, but I want to see how close I can come. And I've made some real close."

Brett will be 40 when his birthday arrives in May. He is in his 19th season in the big leagues, undeniably well into the twilight. If fans are going to jot another 4-3 notation next to his name on their scorecards, it won't be until Brett bolts from the batter's box and barrels toward first base once again for the most basic of reasons.

"It's more fun," he said. "It bothers me when I see young kids billed as superstars don't run ground balls out. It's not fun for me to sit and watch some young kid not run balls out. It can't be fun for the fans, watching young kids not run balls out."

An inspirational style helped Brett become just the 18th player to reap 3,000 hits. But all-round achievement, an ability to do some of everything and do it well, is Brett's full measure.

◆ George Brett started in baseball in El Segundo, Calif., but by 1974 he had donned the major-league uniform of the Kansas City Royals.

K.C. Royals

Consider that Brett has:

- Batted .300 or better in 11 seasons, won three batting championships and is the only player to win them in three decades.

- Scored 100 or more runs four times.

- Twice had more than 200 hits and twice stole at least 20 bases.

- Hit at least 40 doubles in five seasons and at least 10 triples in four.

- Had eight seasons with 20 or more home runs, despite the handicap of Royals Stadium where home runs elsewhere dissolve into long fly balls.

- Drove in 100 or more runs four times.

- Won the American League's Most Valuable Player award in 1980 and won a Gold Glove in 1985 for his defense at third base.

"Of all the people that have come through and are still with the Kansas City Royals, the one most important to our success undoubtedly has been George Brett," Royals owner Ewing Kauffman said.

"Certainly without George, I'm sure the Kansas City Royals would not have won six division pennants, two American League championships and one World Series. So we are indebted to George for all the happiness and pleasure he's brought to us throughout the past 20 years."

His bountiful bottom line notwithstanding, Brett's contributions to the Royals go far beyond the field. He developed into the Royals' signature star, the player who more than anyone else personified an entire team. The Royals were fortunate that, as they left their expansion roots and started to win and capture national attention in the mid-1970s, the brightest spotlight was on Brett.

"He helped in large measure to create the character of the organization," said John Schuerholz, formerly general manager of the Royals and now the Atlanta Braves' general manager. "If he was a jerk or if he was a bad guy or an anti-management guy or a surly guy or a sourpuss or a confrontational person, that's the kind of attitude young players coming through a system to a major-league club begin to take on because that's what the star does.

"There are a number of teams who had that problem — where their star player was not a pleasant person. George was completely the opposite. He's very pro-organization and has a charming and enjoyable personality. I quite frankly miss being around the guy."

SPANNING AN ERA

The Royals drafted Brett in 1971 out of El Segundo High School in El Segundo, Calif. When he went off to Billings, Mont., to launch his professional career that summer, the arbitration process that irrevocably changed the financial landscape of the major leagues was still two years away.

Early in the 1974 season, Brett was in the big leagues to stay. That was two years before the arrival of free-agency, which coupled with the owners' largess began showering multiyear contracts upon the players.

Brett spans baseball's current era, even transcends it. Batting gloves, standard issue for most players today, are tolerated by Brett only in batting practice because "after 19 years my hands are beat up a little bit."

Feeling the bat in his hands is vital to Brett. Except the union is not just that of northern ash and callused skin. Brett has pine tar — just a dark brown, sticky liquid and offstage in the on-deck circle until Brett ushered this substance into the national spotlight and baseball lore — smeared about two-thirds of the way up his bat.

Before settling in the batter's box, Brett, with his right hand, pats the area just above his bat's label for a last daub of pine tar. Several fingers on each of his hands typically are taped.

"I get these little splits and little cuts, and they hurt so bad when you get pine tar and rosin and dirt in there," Brett said. "Whenever one pops up, I put some tape over it, put some cream on it and when it heals, I take the tape off. It's just like a never-ending thing for me throughout the summer."

Tape isn't the only residue of this continual mix of flesh and pine tar. Brett will habitually reach for the top of his helmet with his left hand, sometimes after every pitch, making sure it's secure.

The batboys know better than to wash Brett's helmet, so while his teammates' are always bright blue and clean, Brett's helmet has no sheen. Instead, it is crowned by a brownish smudge, evidence of sweat and toil while mining for hits long enough to reach 3,000.

"It's not a beauty contest out there," Brett said. "It's not a fashion show. This is a war. You don't look good in a battle.

"I used to take grief for wearing my uniform the way I did when I wore my pants real low and my socks real high. I was one of the few guys that did it. Everybody said, 'God you look terrible out there.' I don't care what I look like. It's what I play like."

Brett couldn't care less about styling, the baseball term for the fashion conscious wanting to look spiffy in uniform. He seems connected to an earlier time. Crow's-feet around his bright blue eyes give him the look of an old salt, a venerable touch of age from scrutinizing

Joe Ledford

pitch after pitch after pitch.

"Baseball history shows black-and-white pictures of Gehrig and Ruth," said former Royals reliever Dan Quisenberry, a teammate of Brett's for 10 seasons. "It's almost like you can put George in a picture like that. Give him an old baggy uniform with the socks high, and he would fit in with those guys.

"He'd fit in with those great Yankee teams of the '50s, with (Mickey) Mantle and Billy (Martin) and Whitey (Ford). You could throw him on those teams, and he'd fit. And he fits in today's game. Now he's an old war-horse, really, but he fits with the best."

A BROAD BACK

The Royals used to joke among themselves about their dependence on Brett as the games dwindled and became more crucial. Was Brett's back wide enough to carry the team, catcher Jamie Quirk would wonder while prancing around the Royals' bullpen like a cowboy riding a horse.

Brett was in the forefront when the Royals made it to the American League playoffs for the first time in 1976. His three-run home run against Grant Jackson in the eighth inning evened the score 6-6 in the decisive fifth game with the Yankees. Heartbreak followed for the Royals when Chris Chambliss homered in the bottom of the ninth, giving the Yankees a 7-6 victory and another pennant.

In game three of the 1978 playoffs, Brett hit three home runs against Catfish Hunter at Yankee Stadium, but the Royals lost 6-5 and fell to the Yankees in four games.

Brett ensured a different outcome in 1980. The Royals, winners of the first two playoff games, were losing 2-1 after six innings of game three at Yankee Stadium. When Willie Wilson doubled with two outs in the seventh, Goose Gossage relieved Tommy John.

Gossage was 29 and in his ferocious prime. He had a career-high 33 saves that season. In 99 innings, Gossage allowed just 74 hits and 37 walks while striking out 103. He was 6-2 with a 2.27 ERA and hurled fastballs at hitters like some angry Greek god on a mountain top heaving thunderbolts at the heathens down below.

"I'm in the game," said Quisenberry, who relieved Paul Splittorff after 5⅓ innings. "They bring in Goose, the most dominant relief pitcher of the era. In those days, the relief pitchers took cars in. He gets out of the car, and 56,000 Yankee fans go crazy. It's just too loud."

Somehow, U.L. Washington got enough of an inside fastball to bounce a feeble grounder over Gossage for an infield hit. Up came Brett.

"At that time, I didn't know if George hit Goose well or not," Quisenberry said. "He was throwing bullets."

Brett launched the first pitch into the third deck in right field. The Royals were ahead 4-2 and would win by that score. Shock swept the stadium.

"From 56,000 berserk fans, it went to the calmest, quietest, most placid place except for our dugout," Quisenberry said. "All that energy got transferred into our dugout. I still remember the exhilaration of George coming in. Nobody else could do what he just did."

In the hysteria of the dugout, Brett sought out equipment manager Al Zych. "He said, 'Bub, you can quit driving that piece of ... and get yourself a new car,'" Quisenberry said. "We'd just earned ourselves a World Series check. Not only was it a tremendous bomb, but it was a perfect line for the time."

In the World Series, which the Royals lost to the Philadelphia Phillies in six games, Brett hit .375 (nine for 24) and drew attention.

For hemorrhoids, not hitting.

Brett came out of the second Series game in the sixth inning. He had gone two for two and walked. The real explanation for his departure wasn't disclosed at the time. The Royals blew a 4-2 lead in the eighth, lost 6-4 and headed back to Kansas City.

On Thursday, Oct. 16, a travel day in the Series, Brett underwent surgery at St. Luke's Hospital. Word leaked out that Brett's ailment was hemorrhoids.

During the final six weeks of the season, Brett's quest to hit .400 had subjected him to daily media scrutiny. He answered the same questions over and over and over about his chances of reaching that summit.

When the Series resumed, Brett was hit with a barrage of inquiries. Playing with pain took on a new twist. Worse, the unwelcome legacy of that Series never left Brett.

"There hasn't been a day go by in any city we've played in since that day that I haven't heard some hemorrhoid remark," Brett said. "This is spring-training games. This is every regular-season game I've played in since that happened, there isn't some loudmouth by the on-deck circle making remarks about hemorrhoids."

Joe Ledford

FIVE YEARS OR BUST

Brett has heard a lot of cheering for someone who never hit .300 in the minors. He didn't seem destined for greatness at the outset of his career and gave himself a baseball timetable of five years.

"And if I didn't make it to the major leagues in five years, I was going to quit and get a real job," Brett said. "I don't know what it would've been. Construction worker. Bartender. I wasn't really qualified to do much else at that time with no college education."

Gary Blaylock, a former Royals pitching coach, managed Brett at Billings in 1971 in the short-season Pioneer League. He hit .291 with five home runs and 44 RBI. A shortstop in high school, Brett played that position for most of the '71 season, although Blaylock "wasn't convinced he had enough arm to be a top-flight shortstop."

After being spiked in the knee, Brett played some third base, where Blaylock thought he was better suited.

"I was thoroughly impressed with him as a kid and as a guy that liked to play," Blaylock said. "But I wasn't impressed to the point that I thought he'd be a star."

There had been a vague sign of good things on Brett's horizon earlier that year. John Stevenson, 58, still the baseball coach at El

Segundo High, knew his 1971 team was going to be a powerhouse.

Seeking insights into coaching such talented players, Stevenson, in January 1971, had them take the ISAM test, so called because it was devised by the Institute for the Study of Athletic Motivation that two sports psychologists at San Jose State had originated.

The ISAM test gave recommendations on how to handle the individual, and the comment on Brett began: "He has an inclination to be a con man. He needs firm and clear limits." Following the con-man assertion came two final sentences that in retrospect seem stunningly accurate. "He should respond very well to being challenged and should do well under pressure. He should have little trouble playing up to his potential as an athlete."

Flash to ... October 6, 1978, when Brett hit those three home runs against Hunter in the third game of the playoffs ... flirting with .400 for the final six weeks before finishing at .390 ... hammering that Gossage fastball for a three-run home run Oct. 10, 1980, for the AL pennant ... the ninth-inning home run against Gossage in the Pine Tar Game on July 24, 1983 ... the 1985 season, which Brett considers his finest all-round, and game three of the playoffs on October 11, when he homered twice and went four for four and refused to let the Royals lose after they dropped the first two games to Toronto ... hitting .388 after the All-Star break in 1990, finishing at .329 and, at age 37, winning a third batting title.

Physical talent alone doesn't explain Brett's success. Quirk, a catcher for the Oakland Athletics, formerly Brett's teammate and one of his closest friends, said Brett "probably has the best concentration that I've ever seen in my life for 500 to 600 at-bats in the course of a year."

When the need for a hit was critical, Brett summoned something extra. Eleven seasons above .300 and now 3,000 hits are snow-capped statistical peaks. Gaudy figures by themselves don't reveal Brett's ability to deliver in the clutch, a skill that shaped his career.

"He can drive in a run from the parking lot when he's going well," said Royals Manager Hal McRae, a teammate of Brett's for 15 seasons. "Just get him to Blue Ridge Cutoff, and he can get it in."

GETTING THE CALL

That street had no ties to the major leagues when the Royals drafted Brett in 1971. They were in their third season, still playing at Municipal Stadium and wouldn't move into Royals Stadium until 1973.

The Royals had the fifth selection in the 1971 draft, the highest pick they have ever had. They took pitcher Roy Branch, who was 7-0 and had an ERA of 0.59 in his senior season at Beaumont High School in St. Louis.

Branch did make the majors. But not until 1979, when he surfaced with the Seattle Mariners for two games and the 11 innings that proved to be his entire big-league career.

The Royals atoned for the selection of Branch by taking Brett in the second round. On June 8, 1971, the day of the draft, Brett was at a luncheon in El Segundo, being honored with his teammates for winning a state title. Stevenson, the baseball coach at El Segundo, had arranged for a reporter from the *Daily Breeze* in Torrance, Calif., to call him when Brett was drafted.

"He gets the call and comes back and tells me I was just drafted in the second round by the Royals," Brett said. "I knew nothing about the Kansas City Royals. Living in Southern California and them being an expansion team two years earlier, you don't really know much about them. I was real disappointed."

Royals scout Rosey Gilhousen offered Brett a signing bonus of $11,000. Jack Brett, incensed over what he thought was an insultingly low sum for his son, screamed for Gilhousen to leave his house. Brett ultimately received a $25,000 bonus.

He signed one month after his 18th birthday. Stevenson and his wife, Brett's parents and several of his friends accompanied him to the airport for the flight to Billings.

"It's not going away to college where you can come home on weekends if you live two hours from school," Brett said. "This was a long way from home, and I remember as I said my goodbyes, I started walking through the jet walk to the airplane and I started crying. I stood there for a second, wiped my eyes clean and went and sat down."

Blaylock couldn't believe his eyes when he saw Brett. Shoes and socks were required dress on his team. T-shirts were all right. Shorts were fine. Tank tops and thongs were taboos of Blaylock.

Brett showed up barefoot, wearing "some shorts like I'd wear to the beach every day." Blaylock is a stern, no-nonsense type from the Missouri Bootheel.

"Gary kind of pulled me over," Brett recalled, "and said, 'Hey, you're a professional ballplayer now. You wear shoes.' He let me have it pretty good."

Brett was imitating his brother rather than rebelling. In 1966, the Red Sox took Ken Brett in the first round. He was barefoot when he reported to Oneonta, N.Y., in the New York-Penn League. Ken Brett was the fourth player taken in the country. The Red Sox gave him a bonus of $85,000 and probably wouldn't have cared whether he showed up wearing only a raincoat.

"I was Ken Brett's brother to every scout who came and watched me play in high school," Brett said. "I wasn't as good as Ken Brett, but I was always his brother.

"He was such a great player in high school. He could've gone to any college academically and played football or baseball. He was just your All-American stud. I wasn't the All-American stud."

Ken, 44, cast a large shadow over Brett but by no means the only one. John, 46, and Bobby, 42, each played one season in the minors. Growing up the youngest meant Brett was always following in someone's footsteps.

"I wasn't as tough as John," Brett said. "Didn't have the desire to play that John did. Couldn't run as fast as Bobby. Couldn't hit and couldn't field as good as Ken.

"I was always compared to my older brothers by everybody — the coaches, the teachers. Wasn't as good a student as Ken and Bob, but I was better than John. I was always not as good as somebody in the family.

"And I think that's one of the drives that kept me going to earn the accolades, the appreciation from somebody saying: 'Hey, he's better than Bobby at this. He's better than Ken at this. He's better than John at this.' But it didn't happen until after I left (home)."

PROUD FATHER

Brett received little praise from his father, Jack, an accountant with a staunch belief in discipline and rules. In 1980, Brett took dead aim at hitting .400, a summit that hadn't been scaled since Ted Williams batted .406 in 1941. Brett had his average at .400 as late as September 19 but slid to .390 in the final 13 games. With 449 at-bats, Brett came up five hits short and heard his father put a different spin on his dazzling summer.

Joe Ledford

"When I get home, he said, 'You couldn't have got five more hits?' But that's the way he was," Brett said. "He was always very proud, but he wouldn't let on to it. He would just never let me know it. But I would hear it from other people. So it was like a little game we played. I think he knew what he was doing."

Through the years, Jack Brett and Stevenson, George's high school coach, became good friends. The coach shared Brett's results on the ISAM test with Jack — some years before ever revealing them to Brett — so Jack was aware of his son's con-man tendencies.

"George was a fun-loving guy," Stevenson said. "I think Jack was fearful that George would go the wrong direction and end up blowing the ability he had."

Quirk said: "Jack was rough on him, but George never thought he was rough in a bad way. It was, hey, he's my dad; he knows what's better and George listened."

Jack would check the Royals' box score first thing in the morning. A multihit game by Brett brought a little lilt to Jack's day. By contrast, Jack would be muttering if he discovered Brett had gone hitless.

Jack was listening one evening to a game between the Royals and California Angels. The instant Brett was picked off first base, Jack picked up the radio and hurled it to the floor. The radio shattered into small pieces.

Jack Brett never attended any of the 13 World Series games or 30 playoff games Brett played with the Royals. Just before he died of brain cancer in May, Brett, following a game in Texas, flew to California and visited his father in the hospital.

Jack, wearing a respirator, asked Brett the same questions that were foremost all those mornings he opened his newspaper and searched for one box score. How had the Royals done? How many hits for Brett?

"I struck out three times against Bobby Witt," Brett said. "I didn't have the guts to tell him. My brothers began laughing. I said, 'Not very good.'"

A CARD TO CARRY

That succinct summation might have applied to Brett's career had he not come under the tutelage of Charley Lau, the Royals' hitting coach, in 1974. When he began his professional career, Brett held his hands high and his bat vertical, imitating Carl Yastrzemski of the Boston Red Sox.

"I had a bad problem when I hit like Yaz," Brett said. "My first move — I would cock my hand, and the bat was like pointing out to center field. So then my swing was so long, I couldn't generate good weight shift and a lot of times I couldn't get extension."

Lau preached hitting the ball to all fields. Under Lau's tenets, the batter kept his head down and focused on the ball, shifted his weight from his back to his front side and kept tension out of the swing. Lau was a natural teacher and developed lasting bonds with his regular pupils. They knew how much Lau cared about them and, in turn, were devoted to him.

Lau was 50 when he died of cancer on March 18, 1984. As homage to him, Brett has two baseball cards of Lau when he was with the Detroit Tigers and Baltimore Orioles tacked to the side of his locker. Watching "Later With Bob Costas" gave Brett incentive for another tribute. Hearing Costas say he carried a Mickey Mantle baseball card in his wallet made Brett wonder.

"I said to myself, 'Is there anybody that has been such an influence on my life that I should do the same thing?'" he said.

"There was no doubt who came to mind first."

Which is why Brett carries in his wallet a card of Lau when he was with the Milwaukee Braves.

Brett made his debut in the majors August 2, 1973, replacing injured third baseman Paul Schaal. At 20 years, 2 months and 18 days, Brett was the youngest Royal until Clint Hurdle joined the club in 1977.

In the fourth inning of his first game, Brett lined a single to left field against Chicago's Stan Bahnsen. The Royals optioned Brett back to Class AAA Omaha, Neb., on August 14 and recalled him September 3 for the final month of the season. He batted 40 times, came away with five hits and heard little from Lau.

Brett opened the 1974 season at Omaha and hit .266 there in 16 games. On April 30, Schaal was traded to the Angels for outfielder Richie Scheinblum. The Royals recalled Brett from Omaha on May 3 and put him in the lineup the next night.

He was hitting .205 and had had one hit in his last 22 at-bats when the Royals left Cleveland on June 2. On the flight to Baltimore, Lau laid out a plan to Brett.

"He said: 'I think you've got a chance to be a good player. But you've got to change some things, and you're going to have to go with me 100 percent,'" Brett said. "He said, 'We're going to hit every day at 3 o'clock on the road and every day at 4 o'clock at home for the rest of the year, and I don't want to waste my time if you're not willing to do it.'

"I'd seen the work he'd done with Joe Rudi (in Oakland) and Hal. The year before, in '73, Hal couldn't do anything. In '74, Hal was having a decent year. So I'd seen some of the results he had had working with people, and I'm hitting .200. I'm not going anywhere. So it was a very easy decision on my part."

Initially, Lau and Brett were seeking a hand position where Brett's bat would feel comfortable. Out went the high hands and Yastrzemski lookalike stance. Brett's bat, now held more horizontally, was resting on his shoulder, and he was no longer trying to pull pitches. Lau moved Brett off the plate, closed his stance slightly and had him bend down more.

"The objective," Brett said, "was to hit everything from where the second baseman played me to left field and to keep my head down and take my top hand off (the bat)."

The results were immediate, hits on his first two at-bats against Baltimore. Brett and Lau set .250 as a goal that year. When Brett reached .240, Lau moved the goal to .260. At .250, the goal rose to .270. With three games left in the season, Royals Manager Jack McKeon, not pleased with the allegiance and devotion Lau inspired in some players, had Lau demoted to the minors. Brett went hitless in his final 10 at-bats, and his average slipped from .289 to .282.

With the Royals bobbing along in second and 50-46 in 1975, McKeon was fired and replaced by Whitey Herzog. The banished Lau was brought back from the minors. Brett finished the year at .308, the first time he hit .300 in five professional seasons.

BITTERSWEET TITLES

In 1976, Brett won the first of his three batting titles. Each of those championships left an aftertaste and only the third in 1990 was entirely sweet.

Brett and McRae went into the October 4 season finale hitting .331, .002 ahead of Minnesota's Rod Carew. The Twins closed the season at Royals Stadium, adding to the drama.

McRae answered Brett's hits in the fourth and seventh innings with hits of his own. Carew had hits in the seventh and ninth innings and finished at .331.

Brett led off the ninth with a fly ball that left fielder Steve Brye, playing deep, pulled up on. The sun wasn't in his eyes. But the ball landed in front of Brye, took a big bounce off the artificial turf and went over Brye's head. Brett circled the bases with an inside-the-park home run and an average of .333.

McRae grounded to shortstop and finished at .332. He was incensed with Twins Manager Gene Mauch. He contended that Mauch had Brye play deeper than usual on Brett, so a white player

♦ George Brett's batting stroke progresses from stance through launch to follow-through.

Joe Ledford

would win the batting title. Kauffman came into the clubhouse and consoled McRae. Brett, his locker close to McRae's, stood by himself after just winning a batting title.

Brett was all alone again in 1980 but this time because he lapped the field. Milwaukee's Cecil Cooper hit .352 and finished .038 behind Brett. Brett's ascent to .400 coincided with a team-record hitting streak of 30 games that began July 18.

On August 17, in the 29th game, Brett went four for four on a Sunday afternoon against Toronto at Royals Stadium and climbed to .401. Facing Blue Jays pitcher Mike Barlow, who had struck Brett out on his final at-bat Saturday night, Brett sent a 1-2 pitch over the head of left fielder Garth Iorg, who broke in on the ball, for a three-run double in the eighth. Something unimaginable appeared on the Royals Stadium scoreboard: .401.

Carew hit .388 in 1977 but never reached .400 after July 10. This was mid-August. Brett could seemingly hit anything that was moving, even a golf ball.

He proved that while playing at Lake Quivira Country Club in a foursome that included Orioles pitcher Scott McGregor and McGregor's father.

"I already hit my ball toward the green, and I was walking up with my putter in my hand," Brett said. "They were back about 100-120 yards. Scott hit a ball, and as I'm walking they yell, 'Fore,' and I look up and see the ball coming to me. I swung the putter, hit the ball right on the sweet spot and it flew back and landed about five feet from where they hit it.

"I didn't miss anything in 1980. Do it now, it'd probably hit me in the leg. What a difference 12 years makes."

After his big hit against Barlow, Brett fielded what he thought was a preposterous question: Could he hit .400?

"I'm saying, 'There's six weeks to go in the season. Shake yourself. Have a clue. I'm not going to hit .400,'" Brett said.

On August 18, Brett went three for five in Texas, extending his hitting streak to 30 games and raising his average to .404. That day, Brett discovered what the rest of his season would be like.

Radio stations from all over the country deluged him in his hotel room with telephone calls. The media glare would brighten considerably.

"I felt like I was alienated from the team a little bit the last six weeks because of the run for .400," Brett said. "I really think if I would have enjoyed it more, I would have had a better chance to do it. But mentally, I just got worn down a little bit."

Brett peaked at .407 on August 26 by going five for five at Milwaukee. He was at .396 when he left the lineup for nine games from September 7 to 16 because of tendinitis in his right hand. Injuries limited Brett to 117 games, making his career-high 118 RBI that season all the more notable.

On September 19, Brett had two hits against Oakland and nudged his average to .400 one final time. He slipped to .384 by going four for 20. A final 10-for-19 charge in his final six games brought Brett to .390.

Five more hits in his 449 at-bats, and Brett would have hit .400. His father greeted him with that arithmetic, stressing what Brett had failed to do, not what he had accomplished.

"I felt the same way because so much written was about it," Brett said, "and I had so much coverage doing it. The first man trying to hit .400 in 39 years. And then when you don't do it after talking about it for six straight weeks, you feel like you let some people down."

PROVING GROUND

No one could quibble with Brett when, at age 37, he hit .329 and won his third batting championship in 1990. He was slogging along at .200 on May 7 and as late as July 1 was still mired at .256.

After the All-Star break, Brett went into high gear and hit .388 (108 for 276) with 12 home runs and 58 RBI. His principal challenge for the batting title came from Oakland's Rickey Henderson. Both players sat out games in the season's waning days, jockeying for position by deciding which pitchers to play against.

Brett, hitting .328 and leading Henderson by .002, didn't start the Royals' final game in Cleveland. After pinch hitting a sacrifice fly in the fifth, Brett singled in his next at-bat, putting him at .329, and left the game. Henderson didn't get the multihit game he needed and finished at .325.

Only Ted Williams and Honus Wagner were older when they won batting titles. Media critics and callers to talk shows had doubted Brett. He silenced the skeptics, not all of whom were in Kansas City.

"To show everybody that they were a little premature in my aging process was very gratifying," Brett said. "It was fun to prove these so-called experts didn't know what they were talking about. And two years later, I'm still semiproductive. Not as productive as I'd like to be but semiproductive.

"I've always been able to hold emotion in. But when I came back off that flight from Cleveland and met the media at the airport, there was a point there where I had tears in my eyes."

From the 1990 heights, Brett plunged to a career-low .255 last season. He partially tore the medial collateral ligament in his right knee in the 12th game of the year and went on the disabled list for the ninth time. Brett missed 26 games — making it 209 games he lost during those nine stays on the DL —and wore a large brace on the knee upon returning.

He also became a full-time designated hitter, completing his passage on the diamond. Brett weighed the risks and simply decided enough was enough.

"I had five major knee injuries," Brett said. "I don't want to be like Joe Namath and have new knees put in. And I think the time was right for the switch."

After recovering from a slight tear to the same ligament in that right knee in 1987, Brett moved from third base to first base.

"I enjoyed going over there," Brett said. "There was really no pressure on me because I wasn't a first baseman. If I made an error at third base, that was a no-no because I was a third baseman."

Brett's assessment of his play at third base early on with the Royals? Strong arm. Very erratic. Had good range.

"I took a lot of grounders and got some results," Brett said. "It took longer than I had hoped. But I weathered the storm and got the ultimate award as a defensive player."

Namely, the AL Gold Glove he won at third base in 1985. What overshadowed that award was the season Brett considers his best and the Royals' make-believe October that climaxed with their lone World Series championship.

Brett ended the season with a seven-game hitting streak, including home runs in each of the Royals' four final games. He batted .330 and had 30 home runs, 112 RBI, 108 runs and a .585 slugging percentage. That was only good enough for second in voting for Most Valuable Player in the league behind Don Mattingly of the Yankees.

Brett had a satisfaction far greater than the MVP honor. He helped the Royals beat Toronto in the playoffs and St. Louis in the World Series after being down three games to one in both instances.

Brett led the Royals in hitting, averaging .348 in the playoffs and .370 in the Series.

In game three of the playoffs, Brett had what he considers the best game of his career. The Royals lost the first two games in Toronto, extending their postseason losing streak to 10 going back to the final two games of the 1980 Series.

Brett staved off the catastrophe of a third successive defeat. In the Royals' 6-5 victory, he homered twice, doubled and singled in four at-bats. He scored four runs, including the game-winner in the eighth, and drove in three. And with the Royals ahead 1-0 in the third, one out and Damaso Garcia on third, Brett backhanded Lloyd Moseby's grounder down the line behind third base and made an off-balance throw to catcher Jim Sundberg, getting Garcia at the plate.

Quirk and Quisenberry were watching in awe from the Royals' bullpen. After Brett's second home run, a two-run shot in the sixth, tied the score 5-5, Quirk told Quisenberry: "We're in the driver's seat now. George has one more at-bat."

LOAD TO EXPLODE

When the off-season rolled around, Brett received the only Gold Glove he has ever won. That award is on a shelf in the study of Brett's Leawood home. Brett is a little vague where it will end up in the Mission Hills home he and his wife, Leslie, hope to be in for Christmas.

"We go over to my new house," Brett said, "and they're doing a lot of work on the inside of it. I'm saying, 'We're going to make a little trophy case, and I can put my three silver bats there and I can put some other stuff there.' I never, to this day, think that I've won a Gold Glove. Maybe because I'm a DH now and no longer am a defensive player."

Brett has dug in deep in the batter's box, far from the plate more than 11,000 times. He traces small circles with his bat instead of taking actual practice swings, leans back, awaits the pitch and ...

Load to explode.

Before attacking a pitch, Brett has already considered a host of variables starting in the on-deck circle.

◆ **The older Brett got, the harder he worked to stay in shape.**

"I just watch the flight of the ball," Brett said. "See what he's throwing for strikes and what he's not throwing for strikes.

"Granted, I think I get pitched a little different than the guy hitting ahead of me.

"I kind of have an idea if I made an out last time why I made an out — if I pulled off a ball away or if I jammed myself on a ball in. And just try to figure out a game plan according to what I think he's going to throw me.

"Then when I get up there, I just try to relax and see the ball and hope my fundamentals take over. For me, the less I think when I'm in the batter's box, the better I do. When I start saying to myself, 'Well, I think he's going to throw me this pitch here,' that's when I don't perform very well. I just try to see the ball and hope my fundamentals are true that at-bat."

JUST CALL HIM "LOU"

To teammates, Brett is known as "Lou." The nickname stems from the many childhood hours Brett spent watching cartoons. A family friend began calling Brett "Looney Tunes," which was sometimes shortened to "Looney" or shaped into "Loonis Plumis." To this day, Brett's oldest brother, John, never calls him George. It's always Lou.

John once came into the Royals' clubhouse and asked former Royals pitcher Buddy Black, whose locker was near Brett's, "Where's Lou?" After Black's "Where's who?" response and John's explanation, Brett was no longer George to his teammates.

"Lou's not such a bad nickname," Brett said, laughing. "It's better than 'mullet head.'"

Lau, an ardent fisherman, dubbed Brett with that unflattering nickname after Brett once failed to show up for early batting practice. When Lau came into the clubhouse at about 4:30 after a regular hitting session, Brett was sitting at his locker.

"He starts on me," Brett said. " 'Where were you today?' He said, 'You promised me you'd be here every day, you mullet head.' That was it. I was mullet head until the day he died. He never called me anything but mullet head."

Brett's late arrival followed a night when he and teammate Buck Martinez had been in Westport. At the time, Brett was living in Blue Springs. That's where he bought his first home. Blue Springs was near Royals Stadium. Other players lived there. So Brett, with no knowledge of the Kansas City area, gravitated to Blue Springs.

His introduction to Westport came after hearing about Chuck's Steakhouse, which was located where Lynn Dickey's is now.

"I looked up the number in the phone book and called up from Al Zych's office," Brett said. "I said, 'Are you guys affiliated with the Chuck's Steakhouse in California?' It was the same chain. Jamie and I went down there for dinner. The next day I put my house on the market because I'd never been to Westport before.

"I saw this area and saw all these people. And I said, 'What ... am I living in Blue Springs for?' I'm young and single and successful. I was driving a Porsche. I had a house. I said, 'This is stupid.' Put the house on the market and went and looked at a house in Fairway, Kan., a nice little house that cost $50,000. And I started going down to Westport every night because I was young. I didn't know anybody in town with the exception of the ballplayers, and I wanted to have fun."

When Herzog managed the Royals, he warned Brett he would be 40 before he was 30. Nonetheless, Brett was able to play and play well on little sleep.

"It didn't affect me," he said. "Obviously now, I can't do that. When did I find out I couldn't do that anymore? I found out about four years ago. I remember in '85 I was still doing it. Not as much, but I was still doing it."

Quieter evenings are now routine for Brett. He married Leslic in February. She is expecting their first child in March. If Leslie delivers a boy, Brett will name his son Jack after his late father.

These passages through life for Brett have been accompanied by some inevitable changes on the job. He swings at high fastballs he once feasted upon without making contact. Brett knows he has lost some bat speed, and seven home runs are proof his power has diminished.

More important qualities, though, ones that are unrelated to bat speed or arm strength or any situation on field, really, haven't changed in Brett after 19 seasons with the Royals.

"The guy's a first-ballot Hall of Famer," Schuerholz said, "and has never had his head in the clouds. Never."

Umpire Dale Scott's initial game in the big leagues was in 1985 at Royals Stadium. He worked third base. Scott arrived from Omaha, following a path to the majors similar to many of the Royals and found himself a few feet from Brett.

"I got called up from Omaha," Scott said. "I'm a nervous wreck. He runs out there. I'm trying to stand there and look like I knew what I was doing.

"He says, 'How you doing, Dale?'

"I said, 'Hi, George.'

"He says, 'First game, huh?' "

Seven years later, Scott still laughs hard at Brett's next line.

"He goes, 'Is there a wet spot?' He talked to me like I'd been there 100 years," Scott said, "and believe me the players don't do that. They do the opposite. They try to intimidate.

"It set me at ease before the first pitch was ever thrown. I'll never forget that."

Reliever Steve Shifflett grew up in Pleasant Hill idolizing Brett. On July 3, 1992, they became teammates when Shifflett arrived from Omaha. Two days later, Shifflett was on a flight to Boston, making his first road trip in the majors and found himself next to Brett.

"I was just sitting by myself," Shifflett said. "He said, 'Hey, come here and sit.' He talked to me for about 30 or 40 minutes.

♦ **Charley Lau and hard work helped Brett sharpen his batting skills.**

"I was trying to play it off real cool like it's no big thing. I was pretty excited. It helped a lot to getting used to being here."

In 1984, Brett let pitchers Mark Gubicza and Bret Saberhagen, both rookies, stay with him for the first month of the season.

Gubicza was so shy he was still asking permission to use the phone after being in the house two weeks. Not Saberhagen, who regularly wore clothes from Brett's closets.

"Basically what's mine was mine, and what's his was mine," quipped Saberhagen, who was traded to the New York Mets in December. "I always remind him he was like a dad to me and 'You're old enough to be my dad.' "

In 1986, Quisenberry advised younger Royals to talk to McRae. It was clear that 1987 would be McRae's swan song. Listen to him, Quisenberry said, ask him questions, talk to him about being a big leaguer.

Quisenberry left the Royals in 1988 and retired one month into the 1990 season. Just as he did in 1986 with McRae, Quisenberry would again have a message about the need to pay attention, this time to Brett.

"If I were a Royal today," Quisenberry said, "I'd say to the young guys, 'Hang around this guy. Ask him questions. Look at those hands. Look at those eyes. And watch how he walks to the plate.'

"There's going to be a day when we don't see it any longer. Once he's not on the flights and not in the buses, it's too late for the baton to be passed. There's everything to be gleaned. The whole Royals tradition is right there." ♦

♦ His ability to put a bat on a ball turned Brett into a baseball superstar. (1980 photo)

Jim McTaggart

RISING TO STARDOM

1971◆1980

In the beginning, George Brett was known because of his brother.

It wasn't as if Brett were completely unknown coming out of high school in 1971. Clearly he caught the eye of major-league baseball scouts as he finished his high school career in El Segundo, Calif. That's why the Royals drafted Brett in the second round of the amateur free-agent draft, putting him among the top 40 players picked.

But the first mentions of Brett in Kansas City invariably tied him to his brother Ken, a major-league pitcher. It took a while for Brett, who started his minor-league career as a shortstop, to escape his brother's shadow.

Brett never had a .300 season in the minors, and his first trip to the American League was hardly auspicious. In 13 games and 40 at-bats in 1973, Brett got five hits — a .125 average.

In fact, Brett and the Royals grew up together. Brett won his first batting title in 1976, the first year the Royals won a division title.

Brett continued to develop into baseball's most feared clutch hitter as the Royals added two more division titles.

1980. That was the year the Royals first advanced to the World Series. Not coincidentally, Brett's .390 average — the highest average in the major leagues since 1941 — carried him to the American League's Most Valuable Player award.

Brett already was a star, already was a superstar. That season, as he teetered on the brink of a .400 average for the last two months of the season, made him baseball's most celebrated figure. ◆

TRADITION FAVORS ROYALS IN CHOICE OF PREP STAR

By DEL BLACK

June 9, 1971

Tradition appears to be on the Royals' side in their selection of Roy Branch as their first choice in the major-league baseball draft. And as Lou Gorman, Royals' director of scouting, and 10 members of his staff believe, this young athlete has more than tradition upon which to rely.

Branch is a 17-year-old right-handed pitcher from Beaumont High School in St. Louis. Ten Beaumont graduates have made it to the major leagues. They are: Bud Blattner, Chuck Diering, Bobby Hofman, Jack Maguire, Jim Goodwin, Roy Sievers, Bob Wiesler, Lloyd Merritt, Lee Thomas and Bob Miller. Blattner, of course, is an announcer for the Royals.

Along the managerial trail, Earl Weaver of the Baltimore Orioles is a product of Beaumont.

Gorman and 10 Royals' scouts laid the groundwork for the first-round selection of Branch, a 5-11, 180-pound right-handed pitcher. He's the player they wanted and he

◆ **Brett made his major-league debut two years after being drafted.**

was available when the Royals drafted fifth yesterday in the first round of the regular phase of the draft in New York.

Branch, who also plays third base and carries a .340 batting average, was an all-Metro quarterback in St. Louis last year, the first time a Negro has been chosen the top quarterback in the city. Selection as all-district Back of the Year and honorable mention for Missouri All-State also belong to Branch, who has received 16 football and 10 collegiate baseball scholarship offers.

Kansas City pegged 10 other players yesterday during the first of two days of drafting.

George Brett, brother of pitcher Ken Brett of the Boston Red Sox, was the Royals' second choice. An 18-year-old shortstop from El Segundo (Calif.) High School, young Brett bats left-handed, stands 6 feet and weighs 160. "He has good hands and a good bat," Gorman says. "We believe he will be a good line-drive hitter with power." ◆

MINOR LEAGUE STATS

YEAR	CLUB	AVG.	G	AB	R	H	2B	3B	HR	RBI	BB	SO	SB
1971	Billings	.291	68	258	44	75	8	5	5	44	32	38	3
1972	San Jose	.274	117	431	66	118	13	5	10	68	53	53	2
1973	Omaha	.284	117	405	66	115	16	4	8	64	48	45	3
1974	Omaha	.266	16	64	9	17	2	0	2	14	6	1	1

FAMILY
BRETT'S FATHER REMAINS SON'S BIGGEST SKEPTIC

◆

By BOB NIGHTENGALE

March 6, 1986

FORT MYERS, Fla. — Jack Brett was home one evening listening to the Royals-California Angels game on the radio when he heard the announcer say that his son, George Brett, had just been picked off first base. He grabbed the radio with one hand and, with all his might, threw it against the floor, watching it shatter into tiny pieces.

"Being picked off first base is a bad mistake," Jack Brett said. "It means you have your head up your rear end. He was probably standing on first base thinking how great he was.

"I know he can't win every game. I know he can't bat 1.000. But, when I see him strike out with the bases loaded, or not get a hit when they need one, I say, 'Ah, ...'

"So you watch Johnny Carson and try to make yourself a little happy before you go to bed."

George Brett has been trying to please his father since the day he was born. It probably is impossible to ever satisfy him, but even today, George keeps trying. Every hit he gets, every game he wins, every award he receives, they all are to please one person — his father.

"You have to have some eternal drive, no matter what the subject is," George said. "And with me, it's my father.

"When I'm in the shower after a game, or driving home from the ballpark, I think about how my dad's going to be happy when he gets up and sees the paper the next morning. But if I do badly, he'll throw the paper or his coffee cup against the wall. It'll ruin his day.

"I just think he wants me to do well, so bad that it frustrates him that he can't control it."

Jack Brett never has attended a World Series game. He never has been to any of the 30 playoff games George has played. Instead, he sits at his Manhattan Beach, Calif., home and watches and listens.

"It would have been crowded this year, and all of the rooms and hotels were probably taken," said Jack Brett, who is a finance director for a Datsun associate. "Plus, you can see so much more on TV. You can watch and listen to the announcer. If you sit in the stands, you hear people saying, 'If he makes that much money, why can't he hit?'"

So Jack Brett watches his son from a distance, staying hidden from the attention. He is well aware that George may be one of the finest players in baseball, and a likely candidate for the Hall of Fame, but still there is yet to be a day that he has praised him.

"You've got to understand," Jack Brett said, "I'm not an open person when I come to my feelings. I'm sort of stoic. I think with a friendly look, a little smile, and the nodding your head, you can show your affection.

"If he hit 400 homers in a row, I would not say anything to him. I would not say anything to anyone. I would just nod my head. I make it a point never to talk about George. Never. My attitude is, 'He had a great game, but he was lucky.'

"I read somewhere that the only thing that separates a .330 hitter from a .275 hitter is one hit a week. Geez, does that make him a great person? Does that make him a star? I guess it does."

The house on Penn Street in El Segundo, Calif., was visited almost daily by pro baseball scouts and college coaches. There was the time when Casey Stengel came by. And Yogi Berra. And Carl Hubbell.

Everyone wanted Jack Brett's son. No, not George. It was Ken.

"Ken was as outstanding in high school as George is in his paid profession," Jack Brett said. "That's how great Ken was in high school. Gosh, could he play."

On the mound at El Segundo High School, Ken's record was 33-3. At the plate, he batted .484. Even at the age of 10, Jack Brett said, Ken hit two homers over a 220-foot fence.

Ken was Jack Brett's boy. He was the one who was going to make $1 million a year. He was the one who was going to win the Cy Young. He was the one who was going into the Hall of Fame.

"When anyone looked at the family, Ken was the one," said Bobby Brett, 34, an investment manager who handles George's money. "Ken had great talents. He's still the best athlete I've ever seen come out of this area."

Yet, Ken's professional career was mediocre, at best. He played with 10 teams in 12 years in the big leagues, finishing with an 83-85 record. Never did he win more than 13 games in a season.

"I wanted to cry," Jack Brett said. "I wanted him to be so great. But in the pros, he was just adequate. It still hurts." ◆

◆ Jack Brett had Hall of Fame hopes for son Ken (right) not George. (1976 photo)

The Associated Press

August 3, 1973

Swinging Royals sweep into first

By GIB TWYMAN

CHICAGO — There were no rahs. Nary a sis, boom or a bah. Not so much as one "No.1" shouted in the dressing room. There are too many games left for that.

The Royals climbed to the summit by clawing their way 14 games over the .500 mark at 62-48 with their fifth straight victory in its last 15 games, 20th in its last 28. The Athletics succumbed to the assault on their stranglehold of first by dipping to 60-48 with a .566 percentage, eight points back of the Royals.

But Healy let them waste nothing in the ninth. Lou Piniella laced a single to left and moved to second as Ed Kirkpatrick laid down a perfect sacrifice bunt. George Brett, playing his first major-league game, moved Lou to third with a grounder to first and then Healy came through with his single to center.

It was a textbook inning for acquiring runs of any kind, especially insurance runs. The kind you might expect, really, of a first-place team.

Royals 3, White Sox 1

KANSAS CITY					CHICAGO				
	ab	r	h	bi		ab	r	h	bi
Patek ss	3	1	0	0	Kelly rf	4	0	2	0
Rojas 2b	4	0	3	0	Orta 2b	4	0	1	0
Otis cf	4	1	1	1	Hairston lf	4	0	2	0
Mayberry 1b	2	0	1	0	Melton	4	0	1	0
Hopkins dh	4	0	0	0	May dh	3	0	1	0
Piniella lf	4	1	1	0	Jeter pr-ph	1	0	0	0
Kirkpatrick rf	3	0	0	0	Bradford cf	3	0	0	0
Brett 3b	4	0	1	0	Allen ph	1	0	0	0
Healy c	4	0	1	1	Muser 1b	3	0	1	0
					Alvarado ss	2	1	1	0
					Henderson c	2	0	0	0
					Leon ss	0	0	0	0
					Herrmann c	2	0	0	1
Totals	32	3	8	2	Totals	32	1	9	1

Kansas City	200 000 001 — 3
Chicago	001 000 000 — 1

E: Melton, Leon. **DP:** Kansas City 2, Chicago 2. **LOB:** Kansas City 6, Chicago 5. **2B:** Muser. **3B:** Alvarado. **S:** Kirkpatrick. **SF:** Herrmann.

Kansas City	IP	H	R	ER	BB	SO
Drago (W, 12-10)	5	6	1	1	0	2
Garber (S, 10)	4	3	0	0	0	1
Chicago						
Bahnsen (L, 14-11)	9	8	3	3	3	4

Umpires: Flaherty, Deegan, Springstead, Kunkel. **Time:** 2:28. **Announced attendance:** 11,175.

Fred Blocher

◆ **Brett thought his career might end in the minor leagues.**

BRETT SETS HIS SIGHTS ON 3,000 HITS

◆

By STEVE CAMERON

September 10, 1989

To set the record straight, George Brett did not get a hit on the first major-league pitch he saw.

No, he crashed a line drive straight back at Chicago pitcher Stan Bahnsen, who got his glove up and snared the ball just in time to prevent serious dental damage.

"My first hit was the next at-bat, on a broken-bat single to left," recalled Brett, throwing back his head to laugh. "Charley Lau said, 'I like that stroke.' "

The little business with Bahnsen occurred August 2, 1973, in Comiskey Park.

But the rest of the baseball world took scant notice. Scouts did not fall from their seats, eyes popping, predicting that Brett would stand at first base in 1989, waving to an adoring crowd, celebrating his 2,500th hit.

That happy occasion took place Friday, but Brett recalled how insignificant those early at-bats were considered.

"It's not like I got a hit and started dreaming about 2,500 or 3,000 or anything," he said. "My goal back then was to keep from going back to Omaha. The meal money down there was $4 a day."

In fact, Brett lasted 12 days in the big show. He was back in Nebraska on August 14.

"I don't think people remember that," said Brett, who was recalled in September that first year and wound up hitting a lusty .125. "After my first hit, my only goal was No. 2. Then No. 3. I started the next year at Omaha, too, you know."

This was not a player with huge aspirations.

"I never hit .300 in the minors," he said. "When I first signed, my brother invested my signing bonus and I really thought I'd play three to five years in the minors, and that would be it."

But Brett came to Kansas City for good on May 3, 1974, hit .282 and began drilling the seemingly endless succession of line drives which someday could take him to the Hall of Fame.

Let's dispatch another matter right off: Yes, Brett, 36, intends to swing away for 3,000 hits and, good health permitting, says he'll get there.

"If I hadn't had so many injuries, the six-week or two-month kind," Brett said, "I might not be too far from 3,000 already.

"But hopefully, in another three or three and a half years, I'll get there. I'd like to get 'em all in a Royals uniform." ◆

BRETT BLASTS WAY INTO A MOST ELITE GROUP

◆

By BOB NIGHTENGALE

April 18, 1988

DETROIT — George Brett hit the ball with all his might in the fourth inning Sunday, but instead of running, he stood and watched the ball soar above the upper-deck seats ... above the roof ... until it disappeared.

"I just lost it after that," Brett said.

The ball actually skipped off the Tiger Stadium roof, bounced once on Trumbull Avenue and landed in the Brooks Lumberyard across the street.

It was just the 22nd home run hit out of Tiger Stadium since it was remodeled in 1938 and the first home run to clear the roof since September 10, 1986, when former Tiger Kirk Gibson hit one off Chris Bosio of Milwaukee. It was the first home run hit out of Tiger Stadium by a visiting player since Reggie Jackson did it on May 12, 1984.

"It's the furthest I've ever hit a ball in my life," said Brett, whose homer, hit on a 1-2 fastball off Jeff Robinson, was estimated by Detroit officials at about 450 feet. "I've put a lot into the upper deck at Yankee Stadium, and I hit one in the upper deck in Seattle off Floyd Bannister, but nothing like this.

"I knew the wind was blowing out (24 to 30 mph), and I knew the wind would help it. But I never thought I'd see one go over the roof.

"It's a great feeling to hit a ball that hard, that high, that far. It's a great, great thrill. It's one I'll never forget."

Brett, so excited by the majestic blast, said he almost forgot to run. He stood at the plate watching the ball's flight longer than he can ever remember before beginning his home-run trot.

"Very seldom do I watch my home-runs," Brett said, "and I didn't want to show anyone up. But that one, I just wanted to sit back and enjoy it.

"I feel bad that I did that because I have a lot of respect for the kid (Robinson). I mean, he had a no-hitter going and everything."

Even the partisan crowd of 18,292, as stunned as Brett when the ball disappeared over the right-field roof, was appreciative of the moment. Sitting in silence at the outset, the crowd began cheering Brett as he rounded second. And kept cheering, louder and louder.

"The crowd went crazy," Brett said. "I finally had to go out and tip my hat. I can't ever remember doing that on the road." ◆

May 9, 1974

Royals win as Brett gets first home run

By GIB TWYMAN

ARLINGTON, Texas — Kansas City notched its third straight victory as it began a nine-game road trip by stretching Texas' losing streak to four, longest of the season for the Western Division leading Rangers.

Hal McRae gave the Royals a 1-0 lead in the third inning, singling home Amos Otis from second with one out. Then George Brett, who had gone 3-for-4 in the victory over New York Sunday, hit his first major-league homer in the seventh, a 390-foot drive over the right-field fence that gave Kansas City a 2-0 advantage.

Over the Wall

George Brett hit his longest home run April 16, 1988, at Tiger Stadium in Detroit off Jeff Robinson. Tiger officials estimated the blast at 450 feet. Tiger Stadium opened in 1912, but the upper deck was not added until 1938.

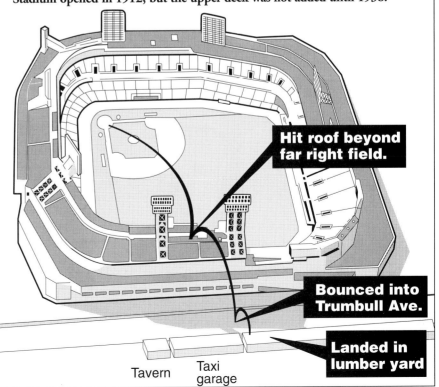

Hit roof beyond far right field.

Bounced into Trumbull Ave.

Landed in lumber yard

Tavern   Taxi garage

Source: Star research, Detroit Free Press, Knight Ridder-Tribune

The Star

♦ Brett (right) edged out teammate Hal McRae and Twins star Rod Carew on the final day of the 1976 season to win his first batting title.

K.C. Star

BRETT'S CLINCHING HIT DRAWS RAGE REVIEWS

◆

By SID BORDMAN

October 4, 1976

Whether it was a conspiracy or not, George Brett captured the American League batting championship on a hit doused with suspicion.

The dramatic finish to the 1976 batting race was an unfortunate twist to a stirring duel by Brett and Hal McRae, both of whom were feeling the heat of Rod Carew until the fifth inning of yesterday's series finale between the Royals and Minnesota.

After Brett's fly ball fell in front of Steve Brye in left field and became an inside-the-park home run in the ninth, McRae grounded to shortstop Luis Gomez for the second out.

With the Twins in front, 5-3, and no extra innings in sight, Brett's average stopped at .333333 and McRae's at .3320682.

As McRae turned to his right and toward the dugout after his final chance to pass Brett, he turned to the Minnesota dugout and showed his disgust. McRae's manifestation of his emotions was directed at Gene Mauch, Minnesota manager.

Mauch bolted from the dugout toward the Royals' side of the field. The umpires and others on both clubs finally contained Mauch.

McRae, who started the final day of the season with less than a percentage point edge over both Brett and Carew, fought back the tears as he took on the inevitable task of talking to reporters.

"Too bad it was like that," McRae said. "I just hope that everybody knows why I lost. I hope that I won't have to explain what happened at home.

"I was glad to see George win, but I'm sorry to see it happen that way. If he got a clean hit, if he just gets a decent hit I wouldn't have been so disappointed. That I lost isn't the big thing. The way I lost is."

McRae, a black, did not mention the word "race," but he did not hide the fact that he felt there were undercurrents.

"This is America and not that much has changed," McRae said. "Too bad in 1976 things are still like that.

"I was surprised that they deliberately let the ball drop in for George. The guy out there played it so well that he played it into a home run. I saw him come in, go back, come in and stop."

Brye, who is rated an average outfielder but one who has been used as a defensive replacement by Mauch, admitted that he messed up.

"I was too deep, I was playing on my own. At first I thought the ball was hit deeper, and I didn't see it real good. I made the mistake."

◆ **Brett received his silver bat in 1977 in honor of his 1976 batting title.**

Mauch, visibly upset over McRae's accusation, said that he imagined that there was some animosity on his club toward the aggressive Royals' slugger. "Hal played tough on our club. But that's the way you're supposed to play. I played aggressively all my life. I would never complain about somebody else.

"This thing hurts me more than anything that has ever happened in my 35 years in baseball. I wouldn't do anything to hurt the game.

"I trust Steve Brye implicitly, and if I felt that he did something dishonest I'd do everything I could to run him out of the game."

Before flying home to Bradenton, Fla., for a couple of days of rest before starting workouts for the playoffs against the Yankees, McRae looked ahead.

"I'm not going to let this affect me in the playoffs or any time," he pointed out. "I shouldn't have let the race get so close. Next year I just have to go out and get a big lead."

Brett, who also led the league with 14 triples and tied for the lead in doubles with 34, rang up his 29th three-hit game and seventh against the Twins this season. He agreed with McRae on his final hit.

"I thought Brye let the ball drop in — but I'm not sure. He was coming hard. I just wish I had hit a line drive and knocked off somebody's glove.

"Really, I wish the thing could have ended in a tie. I got a present from the Twins."

Brett, who finished with 215 hits to set the A.L. pace in that category, too, wanted to win the hitting crown. ◆

BRETT'S SIX CONSECUTIVE 3-HIT GAMES
May 8-13, 1976

DATE	OPP.	AB	R	H	2B	3B	HR	RBI
5/8	at Bal.	4	1	3	0	0	0	0
5/9	at Bal.	5	1	3	0	0	0	0
5/10	vs. Min.	5	0	3	1	0	0	0
5/11	vs. Min.	3	0	3	0	0	0	1
5/12	vs. Min.	5	3	3	0	0	0	1
5/13	vs. Min.	4	4	3	0	0	1	1
6-game totals		**26**	**9**	**18**	**1**	**0**	**1**	**3**

◆ **A game-tying homer in game five of the 1976 playoffs was the first of Brett's 10 post-season home runs.**

NINTH-INNING DRAMA SINKS ROYALS, 7-6

◆

By DEL BLACK

October 15, 1976

NEW YORK — The home run was a double-edged sword for the Royals last night. They lived by it and died by it.

Chris Chambliss drilled Mark Littell's first pitch in the bottom of the ninth inning into the right-center field bleachers to give the New York Yankees a 7-6 victory and the American League championship.

An inning earlier, George Brett's three-run homer rocketed the Royals into a 6-6 deadlock. And back in the first inning, John Mayberry's two-run round-tripper provided Kansas City with a fast start, one that Dennis Leonard, the first of five pitchers, couldn't maintain.

After wiping out the 2-0 deficit in their half of the first, the Yankees overcame a 3-2 Royals' advantage with two tallies in the third inning and climbed to a 6-3 bulge in the sixth, the final run coming on a throwing error by Brett.

Ed Figueroa, the Yankee starter, settled down after yielding three runs on four hits in the opening two innings and permitted only three singles until the eighth.

After being tagged for a leadoff single in the eighth, Figueroa was replaced by south-paw Grant Jackson.

Another Kansas City single preceded Brett's distant shot that tied the game.

Chambliss, who had three hits and as many runs batted in last night, answered the challenge by hammering a Littell fastball for his 11th of the series.

Ironically, Chambliss never touched third and he didn't touch home plate as pandemonium engulfed Yankee Stadium.

By the time the burly first baseman had started his home run trot, thousands among the record Yankee Stadium turnout of 56,821 had stormed the field.

Chambliss might have touched second base, but when he reached third, the base had

◆ **Chris Chambliss**

N.Y. Yankees

Yankees 7, Royals 6

KANSAS CITY	ab	r	h	bi	NEW YORK	ab	r	h	bi
Cowens cf	4	1	1	0	Rivers cf	5	3	4	0
Poquette lf	3	0	0	0	R. White lf	2	2	1	1
Wohlford lf	2	1	1	0	Munson c	5	0	3	2
Brett 3b	4	2	2	3	Chambliss 1b	4	2	3	3
Mayberry 1b	4	1	2	2	May dh	4	0	0	0
Rojas 2b	4	1	1	0	Alomar pr	0	0	0	0
Patek ss	4	0	1	0	Nettles 3b	3	0	0	0
Martinez c	4	0	3	1	Gamble rf	2	0	0	0
					Randolph 2b	3	0	0	0
					Stanley ss	3	0	0	0
Totals	31	7	11	6	**Totals**	37	6	11	6

Kansas City	210 000 030 — 6
New York	202 002 001 — 7

E: Gamble, Brett. **DP:** New York 1. **LOB:** Kansas City 5, New York 9. **2B:** Brett, Chambliss. **3B:** Rivers. **HR** Mayberry (1), Brett (1), Chambliss (2). **SB** Rojas, R. White, Chambliss. **SF:** Chambliss.

Kansas City	IP	H	R	ER	BB	SO
Leonard	0	3	2	2	0	0
Splittorff	3 ⅔	3	2	2	3	1
Pattin	⅓	0	0	0	0	0
Hassler	2 ⅓	4	2	1	3	1
Littell (L, 0-1)	1 ⅔	1	1	1	0	1
New York						
Figueroa	7	8	4	4	0	3
Jackson	1	2	2	2	0	1
Tidrow (W, 1-0)	1	1	0	0	1	0

Time: 3:13. **Announced attendance:** 56,821.

been removed. He had no chance of completing the trek to the plate, being devoured by the fans somewhere near the batter's box.

"I touched where I thought third base should be," Chambliss said.

Later it was reported that police escorted Chambliss to the field and he officially touched the plate.

Manager Whitey Herzog of the Royals was angered by the turn of events, which included a delay before Littell's disastrous pitch because bottles and debris were being thrown onto the field.

Later, Herzog offered congratulations to the Yankees, adding: "They won't be embarrassed by Cincinnati in the World Series."

Leonard failed to get an out in the first inning and was replaced by Paul Splittorff, whose three bases on balls and three hits cost him two runs in the 3⅔ innings he toiled. Marty Pattin worked a third of an inning without incident, giving way to Andy Hassler, who also had trouble finding the plate — walking three — and giving up two hits and a pair of runs in 2⅓ frames.

Mayberry's homer, to the 350-foot mark in right field, with Brett on base after he doubled was the big first baseman's first since August 14 when he connected off Dave Lemanczyk of Detroit at Royals Stadium. It gave Kansas City a 2-0 first-inning lead.

Brett's game-tying blast came after consecutive singles by Al Cowens and pinch-hitter Jim Wohlford.

Cowens opened the eighth with a line drive to left. Grant Jackson, a left-hander, replaced Figueroa.

With Tom Poquette, a left-handed batter, slated to hit, Wohlford grabbed a bat and looped a single to center. Then came Brett's homer, high and deep into the right-field seats. ◆

Joe Coleman

◆ Fred Patek (center) and Amos Otis (left) sit in the dugout after the Royals lost the 1977 American League Championship Series to the New York Yankees.

1977:
BOY, DID THIS ONE HURT
◆

The Associated Press

◆ Brett is attended to after a fight with Graig Nettles in the 1977 ALCS.

It was the most bitter pill.

To this day, George Brett never hesitates. The best team he ever played on was the 1977 Royals.

They compiled a 102-60 record, the best in the major leagues. They won 16 in a row and 24 of 25 in one stretch late in the season. And, the Royals never were behind in the playoff series against the New York Yankees until the very end.

But that's when it mattered. And that's why it hurt.

In the fifth game, after the Yankees scrambled back from trailing 1-0 and 2-1 in the series, the Royals literally fought their way to a 3-1 lead heading into the eighth inning.

Brett was in the middle of the fight, too, of course. He wound up under a pile of Yankees after his aggressive slide into third base touched off combat with New York third baseman Graig Nettles in the first inning.

The Yankees scored a run in the eighth, making it 3-2, but the Royals took the field in the ninth needing only three outs for their first American League pennant. Pitching ace Dennis Leonard entered the game in relief to nail it down.

Instead, it slipped agonizingly away. A bloop single and a walk. A grounder that dribbled through the infield and another bloop hit. Finally, Brett's throwing error, and it was 5-3.

"The Yankees already had gone ahead by then," Brett said. "I was so mad, I didn't even know what I was doing. I almost threw the ball out of the stadium."

The dream died in the bottom of the ninth on Royals shortstop Fred Patek's wicked shot down the third-base line that Nettles turned from a double into a game-ending double play.

"I visualized champagne and staying out until 3 in the morning two days in a row," Brett said afterward. "Now I've got to make plans for the winter." ◆

BRETT: WE'RE NOT OUT OF IT YET

◆

By MIKE DeARMOND

October 7, 1978

NEW YORK — On a three home run day that will burn in his memory for a lifetime, George Brett found himself talking of tomorrow ... of false gods and prophets of doom ... of what might have been but in the end wasn't — again.

In much the same fashion that they had won two previous playoff series with the Royals, the New York Yankees struck late for victory Friday afternoon. This time it was Thurman Munson's two-run home run over the distant left-field wall in the eighth inning that gave the Yankees a 6-5 triumph. New York now has to win either tonight or Sunday to clinch its third straight American League championship.

"It wasn't the fifth game," Brett said, quietly defiant. "There will be a tomorrow. When we lost the fifth games before, then there was no tomorrow. This time there is."

Ron Guidry, the ace of the New York pitching staff stands in the way of that tomorrow, of course. Guidry, 25-3, will oppose Kansas City's Dennis Leonard in Game Four of this best-of-five affair.

"Realistically," Brett said, "Ron Guidry is not God. He is beatable. He's 25-3 and he's the best pitcher in the American League. But if we go out there and play the way we did today we've got a chance to win. And believe me, we're going to play that way."

Brett put Catfish Hunter pitches over the right-field fence on his first three times up. The first one came on the second pitch of the game, giving the Royals a 1-0 lead. Brett's second shot settled into the seats in the third, giving the Royals a 2-1 lead. And the third home run came leading off the fifth, drawing Kansas City into a 3-all tie.

Those were the opportunities the Royals took advantage of. But there were times —

◆ **Jim (Catfish) Hunter**

N.Y. Yankees

Yankees 6, Royals 5								
KANSAS CITY				**NEW YORK**				
	ab	r	h bi		ab	r	h bi
Brett 3b	5	3	3 3	Rivers cf	1	0	1 0
McRae dh	5	0	0 0	Blair cf	3	0	0 0
Otis cf	3	1	2 0	R. White lf	4	2	2 0
Porter c	4	1	2 1	Thomasson lf	0	0	0 0
LaCock 1b	3	0	2 0	Munson c	4	2	3 2
Hurdle lf	4	0	1 0	Jackson dh	3	2	2 3
Wilson lf	0	0	0 0	Piniella rf	4	0	2 0
Cowens cf	4	0	0 1	Nettles 3b	3	0	0 0
Patek ss	3	0	0 0	Chambliss 1b	3	0	0 0
F.White 2b	3	0	0 0	Stanley 2b	3	0	0 0
Braun ph	1	0	0 0	Dent ss	3	0	0 0
Totals	35	5	10 5	**Totals**	31	6	10 5

Kansas City		101 010 020 — 5
New York		010 201 02x — 6

E: Patek. **DP:** Kansas City 2, New York 1. **LOB:** Kansas City 6, New York 2. **2B:** LaCock, Porter, Munson, Otis. **3B:** LaCock. **HR:** Brett (3), Jackson (2), Munson (1). **SB:** Otis. **SF:** Jackson.

Kansas City	IP	H	R	ER	BB	SO
Splittorff	7⅓	9	5	4	0	2
Bird (L, 0-1)	0	1	1	1	0	0
Hrabosky	⅔	0	0	0	0	1
New York						
Hunter	6	7	3	3	3	5
Gossage (W, 1-0)	3	3	2	2	0	2

PB: Munson. **Time:** 2:14. **Announced attendance:** 55,445.

and many of them — that they turned a deaf ear to opportunity's knock.

In the second, Pete LaCock reached third with one down and was stranded. In the third, Kansas City loaded the bases with two down and left 'em loaded. In the sixth, LaCock tripled leading off and couldn't make it home.

"We had the opportunities," said Frank White. "We should have won this ballgame. This game had our name written all over it. But it seems like whenever we get a lead late in the game, something like this happens to us. We needed five outs and we didn't get 'em."

"Last year I came in and struck him out," said Doug Bird, who gave up the homer to Munson that won the game. "Things didn't work out so well this time. I wanted to throw him an out pitch, not a home run pitch. And he hit it out. I'm kind of the butt of things now."

One by one the Royals had their say and one by one they all got around to saying about the same thing.

"We played hard the whole year," said Clint Hurdle. "We aren't going to quit now."

Teammate Paul Splittorff, who pitched 7⅓ innings before giving way to Bird and then Al Hrabosky, allowed as how "It's too bad we didn't win it for George. He had one hell of a game."

But Brett would have nothing of such sentiment.

"It's not what an individual does, it's whether you win or lose," said the Kansas City third baseman. "Even if I go 20-for-20 in the playoffs I don't get a check for $30,000 and everybody else get $10,000. I would rather hit one (home run) and have us win 7-1. I said, 'I hope this isn't a dream,'" Brett noted, recalling his comment after home run No. 3.

And that's the way it might have been.

"It could be a nightmare," Brett added.

And that's closer to what it was. ◆

♦ Brett said he got "goose bumps" from the ovation he received after going over .400 on August 17, 1980.

BRETT SLUGS WAY PAST .400 MARK

◆

By MIKE DeARMOND

DOUBLE SENDS STATISTICIANS SCRAMBLING FOR THE BOOKS

August 18, 1980

Life slowed to the flicker of a silent movie, the ball caught as if in a strobe light, flying in fitful spurts to bounce once short of the left-field warning track, up again off the outfield wall.

A double that swept the bases clean of the Royals. The hit that raised George Brett's batting average to .401.

There will be other games for those on hand at Royals Stadium for Kansas City's 8-3 victory Sunday over the Toronto Blue Jays. There will be other games for George Brett and his teammates in this American League baseball season that still has 45 games to run before the cooling winds of October supplant this muggy month of August.

But this day, this one moment in the eighth inning of an otherwise meaningless game of 1980, will be long remembered by all as nothing less than a game of games and perhaps as much as a harbinger of history.

"Goose bumps," said Brett, Royals' third baseman who has hit in 29 consecutive games and has crossed the .400 batting barrier no man has bettered over the course of a season since Ted Williams hit .406 for the Boston Red Sox in 1941.

Brett's movement past the .400 mark has sent statisticians all around the country scurrying to find the last hitter to breach .400 this late in the season. Since Williams, it is believed the closest was Rod Carew, who was hitting .400 July 8, 1977. Carew, then with the Minnesota Twins and now with the California Angels, dropped off to .388 that season.

The day began for Brett as any other day. Armed with the knowledge his batting average stood at .394, Brett walked down to

Royals 8, Blue Jays 3									
TORONTO					**KANSAS CITY**				
	ab	r	h	bi		ab	r	h	bi
Griffin ss	4	0	1	1	Wilson cf	1	1	0	0
Moseby rf	1	0	1	0	Otis cf	2	1	0	0
Bailor rf	5	1	2	0	Wathan lf	3	2	1	0
Mayberry 1b	4	0	1	0	Brett 3b	4	1	4	5
Velez dh	3	1	1	0	Porter c	4	0	1	1
Garcia 2b	4	0	1	1	Aikens 1b	4	0	1	1
Howell 3b	4	0	2	0	Torres rf	0	0	0	0
Iorg lf	3	0	0	1	McRae dh	4	0	0	0
Ainge cf	4	1	1	0	Quirk rf	2	1	1	1
Whitt c	4	0	2	0	LaCock 1b	1	0	0	0
					Chalk 2b	1	0	0	0
					White 2b	2	1	0	0
					Washington ss	3	1	1	0
Totals	36	3	12	3	**Totals**	31	8	9	8

Toronto	001	100	010 — 3
Kansas City	100	100	33x — 8

E: Chalk, Griffin. DP: Kansas City 1. LOB: Toronto 8, Kansas City 8. 2B: Ainge, Bailor, Brett 2, Moseby. HR: Quirk (5). SB: Wilson, Quirk. S: Iorg, Washington.

Toronto	IP	H	R	ER	BB	SO
Clancy (L, 11-9)	6 2/3	5	5	5	6	4
a-Willis	0	2	0	0	0	0
Schrom	1	1	3	3	2	0
Barlow	1/3	1	0	0	0	0
Kansas City						
b-Splittorff (W, 9-8)	7	9	3	3	1	3
Quisenberry (S, 25)	2	3	0	0	0	0

a-pitched to two batters in seventh.
b-pitched to two batter in eighth.
Time: 3:06. Announced attendance: 30,693.

the Royals' bullpen to hit balls off a stationary batting tee.

Through six innings, in fact, the game was like any other with the minor exception the Royals and Blue Jays were tied 2-2.

Then in the seventh, with teammates Frank White and John Wathan on base with two outs, Brett lined his third consecutive hit on this 4-for-4 day down the right-field line. The hit scored two runs, boosted the Royals into a 4-2 lead they never relinquished on the way to their fifth consecutive victory.

But, more importantly, the hit drove Brett's batting average to .399. Suddenly, the tension, the expectation, began to build.

Would Brett get another chance? Could each and every inhabitant of the park be able to say, "I was there the day George Brett hit the .400 mark?"

"I didn't think I would," Brett said. "I was sixth up, which meant we would have to have the bases loaded when I came up or we would have to have a couple of runs already scored."

The former was the course followed by this unbelievable script.

Pete LaCock flied out to center and White grounded out to short. U.L. Washington beat out an infield hit and Amos Otis walked.

That brought up Wathan.

Ball one produced a slight stirring in the stands. Ball two, and the buzzing hedged to a roar. Ball three brought a reaction Royals' catcher Darrell Porter described as a "who-o-o-o!"

And then, ball four.

The Royals' dugout was, by now, sheer bedlam.

"We were all pulling for him and screaming," said Royals' outfielder Clint Hurdle.

But, after the initial uproar over Brett's purposeful stroll to the batter's box, sight slowly began to obliterate sound.

Mike Barlow, who struck out Brett in Brett's final at-bat Saturday night, was brought on to face the Royals' third baseman.

"When I got to .399," Brett told himself, "I said, 'If I hadn't chased a bad ball last night off of Barlow I probably would be at .400 right now.'

"I told myself not to swing at any bad balls."

Brett took the first pitch. "A good riding fast ball for a strike."

The second pitch was inside for a ball. And then the second strike, a foul, "was one I fished for," Brett said.

The next pitch was the pitch.

Brett ripped it hard to left. At first, the ball appeared catchable. But Garth Iorg broke in, then back toward the fence and by that time it was too late for even the most miraculous of recoveries.

"Usually I hit the ball and just run to first," Brett said. "I think I was peeking a little bit to see if he was going to catch it or not." ◆

WILLIAMS HAS NO EDGE OVER BRETT

◆

By JOE McGUFF

August 20, 1980

As George Brett looks on a world filled with microphones, tape recorders and note pads, he might be surprised to learn there was a time when .400 hitters were taken so lightly the achievement was not even worth one line in a game story.

Bill Terry of the New York Giants finished the 1930 season with a .401 average. The wire-service story carried in *The Times* following the final game of the season merely noted that Terry had failed to break the National League record for hits. The only paragraph concerning Terry read:

"Bill Terry failed to make a hit during the game and remained tied with Frank O'Doul, who established the National League record for hits in 1929 with 254."

So much for Bill Terry and his .401. There had been seven .400 seasons in the previous 10 years and seemingly the media and public had become a bit jaded.

Terry is the last National Leaguer to hit .400, and the only American Leaguer to do so since then is Ted Williams of the Boston Red Sox who batted .406 in 1941.

As Brett enters the closing days of August in hot pursuit of a .400 season, there are two questions of historical significance to be considered: Why has baseball produced only one .400 hitter since 1930, and are conditions more difficult for Brett than they were for Williams in 1941?

The dearth of .400 hitters probably has been caused by major changes in the use of relief pitchers, improved defense and emphasis on the long ball.

The conditions under which Williams hit .406 and those facing Brett today are different, but the pluses and minuses appear to balance out.

Teams were able to bunch their defense against Williams, who was a pull hitter. There is no one way to play Brett because he hits to all fields. Although relief pitching is more of a factor today than in 1941, Brett, like Williams, hits left-handers as well as right-handers.

At this point, Brett would appear to have as good a chance to hit .400 as Williams did 39 years ago. ◆

The Associated Press

◆ **Brett went 5 for 5 in a game in Milwaukee on August 26, 1980, to raise his average to .407.**

BRETT'S QUEST BEGINS TO TRANSCEND GAME

◆

By MIKE DeARMOND

August 19, 1980

ARLINGTON, TEXAS — Monday began for George Brett the way Sunday ended ... the way today began ... the way the coming days will begin and end.

A microphone was thrust in his face. A notebook was shoved under his nose. The eye of a television camera focused on his every move.

"It's becoming a joke," Brett said. "It really is."

Suddenly, the game isn't the thing anymore; what counts is Brett's batting surge. The Royals' All-Star third baseman is more than halfway to Joe DiMaggio's 56-game hitting streak, with a string of 30. And his batting average is .404, a level nobody seemingly attains in the third week in August.

Despite the feats of others and the team accomplishments, the subject is Brett — before, after and during the game.

"It's a big thing, but it's not a big thing," said Brett. "What I mean is ... have I said this before? ... I'm not going to put pressure on myself. How many times have I said that?"

"About 20," he was told.

"It's fun," Brett said. "It kinda is," he amended. "I'm just starting to get it (the crush of interviews)." ◆

30-GAME HITTING STREAK
JULY 18 - AUGUST 18, 1980

DATE	TEAM	AB	R	H	2B	3B	HR	RBI	AVG
7-18	at NY	5	1	4	0	0	1	4	.377
7-19	at NY	5	1	2	1	0	0	2	.377
7-20	at NY	4	0	1	1	0	0	3	.375
7-21	vs. Chi	3	0	2	0	0	0	0	.379
7-22	vs. Chi	4	0	1	0	0	0	0	.377
7-23	vs. Chi	5	2	2	1	0	1	1	.377
7-24	vs. Chi	4	1	2	0	0	0	2	.379
7-25	vs. NY	3	0	1	0	1	0	1	.379
7-26	vs. NY	4	0	1	1	0	0	2	.377
7-27	vs. NY	5	0	1	0	1	0	2	.373
7-29	vs. Bos	5	4	4	2	0	1	1	.382
7-30	vs. Bos	2	0	2	0	0	0	1	.386
7-31	vs. Bos	3	2	2	0	0	0	1	.390
8-1	at Chi	4	0	1	0	0	0	1	.388
8-2	at Chi	5	1	2	0	0	0	0	.388
8-3	at Chi	4	0	1	0	0	0	0	.386
8-4	at Det	4	1	1	0	0	1	1	.384
8-5	at Det	3	1	1	0	0	1	3	.383
8-6	at Det	4	2	2	0	0	1	1	.385
8-8	at Tor	4	1	2	0	0	0	2	.386
8-8	at Tor	3	1	2	1	0	0	0	.389
8-9	at Tor	5	0	1	0	0	0	1	.386
8-10	at Tor	5	2	3	1	0	0	1	.390
8-11	vs. Bal	4	0	1	0	0	0	0	.388
8-12	vs. Bal	4	1	2	0	1	0	1	.389
8-13	vs. Bal	4	0	2	0	0	0	1	.391
8-15	vs. Tor	4	1	1	0	0	1	3	.389
8-16	vs. Tor	4	2	3	0	0	0	2	.394
8-17	vs. Tor	4	1	4	1	0	0	5	.401
8-18	at Tex	5	3	3	0	0	0	0	.404
Totals		**122**	**28**	**57**	**9**	**3**	**6**	**42**	**.467**

AS DAYS DWINDLE, BRETT DRAMA BUILDS

◆

By MIKE DeARMOND

September 17, 1980

He pulls a batting helmet to the tops of his ears, yanks a bat from the rack and strides to the center of his world.

Arriving at the plate, he taps the dirt from his cleats and breaks the rhythmic sway of his batting stance, driving the baseball past an infielder, over an outfielder, sometimes over the fence.

The vision runs countless laps around the inside of George Brett's head.

Tuesday, though, the reality again was that of the helmet remaining on the dugout steps and the bat staying in the rack. The only striding Brett did was to traverse the short distance from the water cooler to his locker.

For most Royals, the Tuesday night rainout of the scheduled game against California was a rare second straight day off. For Brett, it was his 10th day off since tendinitis in his right wrist sidelined him September 7 in Cleveland.

Another 10 days out of the lineup is something Brett can ill-afford if he hopes to become the first man since Ted Williams in 1941 to hit .400 or better in the majors.

Brett knows he can't sit idle much longer.

"If I miss this home stand (six games against California and Oakland, winding up Sunday), it would be very, very tough," Brett said. ◆

◆ **His race for .400 and the Royals' appearance in post-season play made Brett the center of media attention in 1980.**

BRETT: PRESSURE GOT TO BE TOO MUCH

◆

By MIKE DeARMOND

BECOMING FIRST .400 HITTER IN 39 YEARS BECAME 'YARDSTICK' FOR SEASON

October 1, 1980

For more than a month he had been saying it. Over and over and over again. Each day. Every day. George Brett was not going to put any pressure on himself.

And then, on the Royals' last road trip — an 0-6 swing through the all-too-real never-never land of defeat — Brett awoke to the realization he had done that very thing.

The quest to become baseball's first .400 hitter in four decades was fading away. And Brett cared, more than he had ever wanted to admit, even to himself.

"I was a basket case on the last road trip," Brett said Tuesday night before the Royals' game against the Seattle Mariners.

Brett has always prided himself on a loosey-goosey approach to baseball. Let others approach the sport as a job; Brett saw it as a game. Zero for four nights at the plate rolled off his back like wind off the surf in Brett's native California.

Only suddenly, as a 3-for-20 string dropped Brett's batting average to a mere .384

after an 0-for-4 game Saturday morning in Minnesota, Brett realized he cared too much.

"I wanted it bad," Brett said. "But I wanted it too bad. I still want it bad, but I'm not going to change my life for it. This is a year I should have enjoyed more than any other in my life. But I didn't enjoy it at all."

The quest for .400 did that. It became more than a part of a wonderful season. It became the yardstick. All or nothing.

Brett now, once again, is able to take whatever comes.

"It's out of reach," Brett said of hitting .400, "but it's not over." ◆

◆ Brett's homer off New York's Goose Gossage in the 1980 playoffs carried the Royals to their first pennant and exacted revenge for three playoff series losses to the Yankees.

ROYALS HEAD FOR FIRST WORLD SERIES

◆

By MIKE FISH

BRETT'S HOMER DECISIVE

October 11, 1980

NEW YORK — The Royals have captured the magic of New York.

"Neither a wild, screeching Yankee Stadium crowd nor ace relief pitcher Rich Gossage could save the Yankees from the Royals this time. The frustration is over."

George Brett sealed the Royals' first American League pennant with a three-run homer into the upper deck in right field. The Royals swept their old nemesis in three games of the American League Championship Series, punching their ticket to the World Series with a 4-2 come-from-behind victory Friday night.

So much for the bitter memories of '76, '77 and '78.

"I just tried to pull it and get it up in there," Brett said of his seventh-inning blast. "Defeating the New York Yankees is the biggest obstacle in our lives."

Brett's dramatic home run, a record-tying sixth in playoff competition, was the offensive blow that snapped the Yankee jinx.

"They're gonna go crazy out there (Kansas City)," said Brett. "There's real dislike between the two cities. It's a tremendous rivalry.

"It's just something they deserved. They've experienced so much frustration ... all I know is I feel a lot happier than in '78. When I hit that I knew the game was over."

It's off now to either Houston or Philadelphia for the Royals.

But game three didn't come easy. The Yankees made a mad dash, loading the bases with none out in the eighth.

The Yankee Stadium crowd of 56,588 was on its feet, screaming and clapping in wild frenzy. Bob Watson started the threat with a triple that scooted past Amos Otis into the left-center gap. From there, reliever Dan Quisenberry loaded the bases with walks to Reggie Jackson and pinch-hitter Oscar Gamble.

Quisenberry, who has survived all season on the double-play ball, got behind Rick Cerone in the count 2-and-1. But the Yankee catcher lined the next delivery to shortstop U.L. Washington, who threw to second, doubling up Jackson. Pinch-hitter Jim Spencer grounded out to second, killing what would be the last Yankee threat.

"It feels good," said second baseman Frank White, the series Most Valuable Player. "Those three years we lost here we had to go back, drink our beer and sort of drink our tears. Three in a row just makes it sweeter.

"It's just an incredible feeling. You could almost hear the crowd silence when George hit that homer. You could hear their hearts die."

Quisenberry pitched the final 3⅔ innings, earning the victory. In the end it was the slender right-hander against his well-publicized rival — Goose Gossage.

Gossage's long-awaited appearance in the series didn't come until two were out in the Royals' seventh. He came on after starter Tommy John surrendered a double to Willie Wilson and an infield hit to Washington.

It was the classic confrontation — Brett against Gossage, power vs. speed.

But Brett made a shambles of the challenge when he drilled Gossage's first pitch a dozen rows deep into the right-field upper deck. ◆

◆ **Teammates knew Brett's homer meant they were going to the World Series.**

◆ **Brett told reporters that "defeating the New York Yankees was the biggest obstacle in our lives."**

♦ The Royals gather at Kennedy International Airport to watch the end of the 1980 playoff game between the Houston Astros and the Philadelphia Phillies so they could determine which city to fly to on the charter.

♦ Brett's only World Series home run came in the third game.

♦ Each team had a future Hall of Famer at third base in the 1980 World Series: Brett of the Royals and Mike Schmidt of the Phillies.

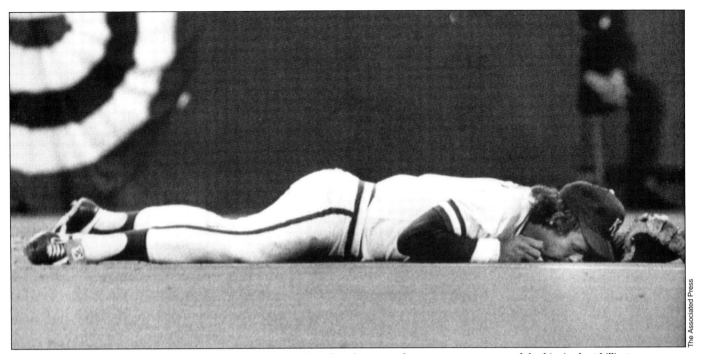

♦ Game five proved to be the turning point of the Series. Mike Schmidt's grounder past Brett was one of the hits in the Phillies' game-winning rally in the ninth inning.

♦ Brett got only three hits in 11 at-bats after Dickie Noles of the Phillies knocked him down in game four. (above and right)

1980
WORLD SERIES
◆

GAME 1 - Oct. 14
Philadelphia 7, Kansas City 6

GAME 2 - Oct. 15
Philadelphia 6, Kansas City 4

GAME 3 - Oct. 17
Kansas City 4, Philadelphia 3

♦ Brett's stature as baseball's best hitter made him the focal point of media attention.

♦ A line-drive hit by Pete Rose in game six was one of the blows that clinched the Series for the Phillies.

♦ Brett batted .375 in his first World Series.

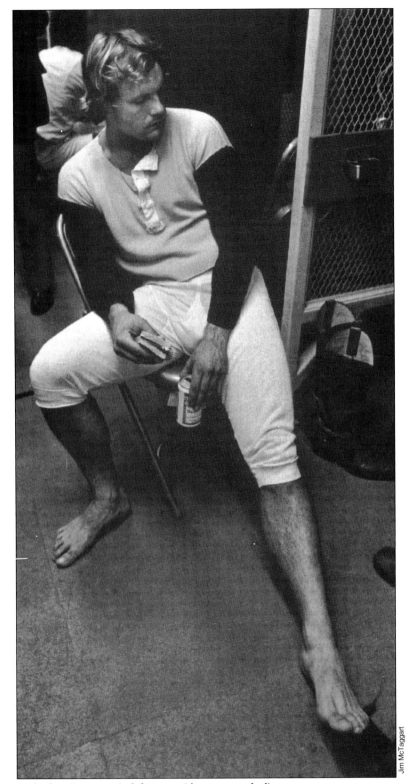

Jim McTaggart

◆ The loss in game six left Brett with an empty feeling.

K.C. Star

◆ Brett and the Royals found reason to celebrate after the World Series in 1980, but they would have to wait five years to bring the title home.

1980
WORLD SERIES

◆

GAME 4 - Oct. 18
Kansas City 5, Philadelphia 3

GAME 5 - Oct. 19
Philadelphia 4, Kansas City 3

GAME 6 - Oct. 21
Philadelphia 4, Kansas City 1

WHY ME? WHY NOT JOE McGUFF?

◆

By JOE McGUFF

October 17, 1980

After a wait of 26 years, the World Series has come to Kansas City, but it has arrived in damaged condition.

George Brett, suffering from the world's most widely covered case of hemorrhoids, is in St. Luke's Hospital for treatment. He rested on the charter flight home from Philadelphia by stretching out across three seats in the coach section. Brett was in pain and for that matter so were the Royals.

Until Tuesday everything had seemed so easy for them. They won the American League West from here to Seattle. They won the American League Championship Series from the New York Yankees in three games and left a sulking George Steinbrenner working on a Yankee hit list.

Now, for the first time this season, the Royals are dealing with adversity. They trail the Phillies two games to none and if they lose Friday night at Royals Stadium, the tournament to determine the best team in the world of Bowie Kuhn will be all but over.

The Royals also need to get Brett back in the lineup. He left the game in the sixth inning Wednesday night after getting two hits and drawing a walk against Steve Carlton, the Phillies' best pitcher. His status for the third game probably will be in doubt until shortly before game time.

It is ironic that Brett, widely acclaimed as the best hitter in baseball, might be forced out of his first World Series by an ailment everyone jokes about except the sufferer. Brett said he is frustrated, but still hopes to play.

"I just want to get the damn things taken care of," Brett said.

"I've done everything they've asked me to do. I feel disgruntled. I keep saying, 'Why me? Why not Joe McGuff?'"

Brett grinned wryly and added, "I'm going back to the same room I always have at the hospital. I've had it five years in a row."

If the Royals are looking for encouragement, perhaps they can draw on the fact that the World Series of 1980 has a look of unpredictability.

After all, who could guess that three days into the Series the nation's columnists and baseball writers would be interviewing not Pete Rose or Mike Schmidt but a proctologist. In a World Series that has brought hemorrhoids out of the closet, almost anything is possible. ◆

◆ Brett talks with reporters in the clubhouse after game two of the 1980 World Series against the Philadelphia Phillies. Brett left the game in the sixth inning after going 2-for-2 with a walk. It was later revealed he was suffering from hemorrhoids.

Jim McTaggart

♦ Neither Brett nor Jimmy Carter won election as president in 1980, but Brett did win the MVP award.

BRETT IS AL'S MVP

♦

By MIKE FISH

November 19, 1980

George Brett is everything a manager would ask for in a Most Valuable Player. He just wasn't in the lineup as often as previous recipients.

Tuesday, the Baseball Writers' Association of America chose the Royals' All-Star third baseman as the American League's Most Valuable Player. In the future, however, baseball historians will recall him as the Band-Aid player, a training room miracle.

No non-pitcher has ever missed more games (45) than Brett and been acclaimed as his league's best. Not Mantle. Not DiMaggio. Not Mays.

And only the late Gabby Hartnett, who hit .344 in 116 games with the Chicago Cubs in 1935, won the award while playing in fewer games than Brett's 117.

But Brett's playing time or lack of same did nothing to cloud this, the latest and most prestigious of post-season awards.

"It's like the Cy Young if you're a pitcher. This is the one I really wanted," said Brett, who finished ahead of Reggie Jackson and Goose Gossage of the New York Yankees, second and third, respectively, in the AL voting. Royals' teammate Willie Wilson finished fourth and the Milwaukee Brewers' Cecil Cooper fifth.

"There's a little anxiety, you don't want to build your hopes too high," said Brett, vacationing in Palm Springs, Calif. "I remember one year (1976) I thought I had a good chance at it and didn't win. That

left me a little upset. Thurman (Munson of the Yankees) got it. So I learned not to be too confident about winning."

When baseball historians look back at Brett's accomplishments, they likely will zero in on his .390 batting average — the highest since Ted Williams hit .406 in 1941 — and his 118 RBI in only 117 games. But the story may be hidden in the number of games he missed.

Brett compiled figures overall that no American League player accomplished while playing every day. And his statistics — .390, 24 home runs, 118 RBI — are career highs.

He is the youngster who missed a fair portion of school and then jumped to the head of the class with a report card full of A's. He is the American League's valedictorian for 1980, the premier player of the game. ♦

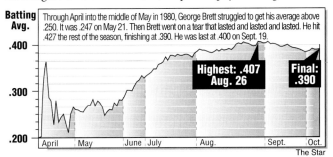

Batting Avg.

Through April into the middle of May in 1980, George Brett struggled to get his average above .250. It was .247 on May 21. Then Brett went on a tear that lasted and lasted and lasted. He hit .427 the rest of the season, finishing at .390. He was last at .400 on Sept. 19.

Highest: .407 Aug. 26

Final: .390

The Star

◆ Brett hugs Bret Saberhagen near the mound after the Royals beat the St. Louis Cardinals in the seventh game of the 1985 World Series in Kansas City. The victory gave the Royals their first World Championship.

Keith Myers

◆ **Brett is covered with shredded paper during a parade celebrating the Royals World Series Championship in 1985.**

WINNING IT ALL

1981◆1985

That, George Brett will tell you, is his biggest moment in baseball, hugging Bret Saberhagen after the last out of the 1985 World Series.

Of course, they wouldn't have bothered to hug if the Royals hadn't won it all. And, of course, the Royals wouldn't have won it all, or come close for that matter, if it hadn't been for Brett.

After the 1980 World Series loss to the Phillies, who would have thought it would take the Royals five seasons before they won another American League pennant?

Brett followed his stunning 1980 season with a mere mortal .314 season in 1981, a season interrupted by a players'

strike. He hit better than .300 the next two seasons as well, but he dropped to .284 in 1984, a year the Royals rebuilt their team into a division champion around a nucleus of young pitchers.

Brett bounced back in 1985 with arguably his finest season. He hit .335 with 30 homers and 112 RBIs. More to the point, he refused to let the Royals be anything but champions.

Not when they fell 7½ games behind, in last place, in July. Not when they frittered away a three-game lead in September. Not when they fell behind Toronto 2-0 in the American League playoffs.

In fact, the third game of that series is Brett's finest overall performance in

the clutch. Details to come, but reserve catcher Jamie Quirk, who was sitting in the bullpen when Brett bashed his second home run, a two-run blow that tied the game 5-5, put it best. "We're in the driver's seat now," Quirk said. "George has one more at-bat."

He was right. Then, Brett batted .370 as the Royals won the World Series by coming from behind against the St. Louis Cardinals.

"For the first time in my life, 25 guys got together and got to celebrate something very, very special," Brett said, shortly after he announced his retirement. "Winning the World Series is the ultimate for a baseball player." ◆

UMPIRES' RULING BEATS THE TAR OUT OF ROYALS

◆

By MIKE McKENZIE

July 25, 1983

NEW YORK — George Brett laughed. The laughter turned, instantly, to rage. Rage gave over to tears. And tears of frustration and disbelief eventually dissolved into a dispassionate lull.

He touched all bases of a home run of emotions. All because of a home run of infamy.

Eventually, shower-drenched and with time to pacify his swirl of feelings, Brett stood before a world of questioners, shook his head, sighed and said, "If I had any guts I'd retire, because now I've seen it all."

What he had seen at approximately 4:40 p.m., Yankee Stadium time, was a Goose Gossage fastball rising high and far off his bat and into the right-field grandstand, apparently giving the Royals a 5-4 grip on a possible victory with two outs in the top half of the ninth inning.

Moments later he saw home-plate umpire Tim McClelland, after several minutes of confusion and commotion that included using home plate as a measuring rod, step toward the Royals' dugout and signal Brett was out.

The third out. The game, therefore, was over. Two runs on Brett's homer did not count. The Yankees won 4-3.

The pine tar Brett had applied to his bat — to improve grip and prevent blisters, he said — extended higher on the barrel of the bat than the 18 inches allowed by the rules.

Yankees Manager Billy Martin had the umpires check the bat, at the behest of one of his coaches, Don Zimmer.

"I was in the dugout laughing at them," Brett said. "They had no case."

"We had nothing to measure with," Brinkman said later. He used the front edge of home plate, which is 17 inches across. Brinkman said the pine tar extended in thick substance a "good 19 to 20 inches" and in a lighter amount even higher.

Brett lost control when he was called out. He rushed from the dugout toward McClelland. Brett's cheeks puffed in and out, like bellows, as strong words and heavy breaths fought for space around his chew of tobacco. If ever there was a raging bull ...

And Brett's primary epithet of disbelief, witnessed through lip reading on television monitors and surely blistering to the umpires' ears, had something to do with bull. ... It wasn't feathers.

◆ Brett was in the dugout "laughing at them" when the Yankees asked the umpires to look at his bat. After home-plate umpire Tim McClelland called him out, Brett emerged to plead his case.

So, Brett had the ignominious distinction of hitting a game-losing home run, and Gossage got a save by giving up a hit into the seats.

Royals Manager Dick Howser telephoned the American League office to protest the umpires' decision, and today he will send a telegram formally lodging an appeal.

"I can't buy it," Howser said. "Broadway wouldn't buy that script. It wouldn't last past opening night it's so unbelievable. They'll never convince me they're right. I'm sickened by it. Really. Sick to my stomach."

Howser said never in his quarter-century or so of baseball had he ever seen the likes of this ruling. Likewise, Brett. "I've played baseball since I was 8, and I've never seen anything like this. We played by the rules when we were 8."

His misadventure set off a sequence of actions worthy of vaudeville. Rick Cerone, the Yankees' catcher, had been told to grab Brett's bat if Brett got an important hit. A possible game-winner seemed important enough, so Cerone picked up the bat. Then he threw it back down. "I knew it didn't have any cork in it, and couldn't remember why they told me to get it," he said.

The batboy assigned to the Royals (who asked that his name not be used because he might get in trouble) said he took the bat toward the dugout until Cerone yelled for him to bring it back. When he gave it back to Cerone, the youth said, the Royals started yelling at him.

After the umpires had measured and made their call, Royals pitcher Gaylord Perry sneaked behind the scene and grabbed the bat while the umpires were engaged in holding back Brett and arguing with Howser.

Perry gave the bat to Hal McRae, but a uniformed security guard intervened and took the bat off the field. The bat was carried to the umpires' room by a group of guards, one of whom spoke into a walkie-talkie, saying such things as "We've got it, everything's under control. ..."

Howser, brimming with sarcasm to temper his fury, said, "Suddenly I saw guys in sport coats and ties out there chasing the bats. What were they, CIA? Then people were everywhere, clubhouse attendants, people from the Bowery. It was like the Brinks robbery had taken place. Who's got the gold? And where's the bat now, in the think tank at the Pentagon? Oh, the umpires have it — then, no, it's not in the think tank."

Much later, Brett inquired whether he would receive the bat back before departing. "I want to use it tomorrow night," he said. "Best bat I've ever had."

He expounded at great length on the details of why he uses pine tar, anyway. Brett is one of the few batters who doesn't use a glove when he bats. He likes the "feel" of raw bat, he said, and the tar "keeps my hands from getting torn up."

Brett admitted he knows, however vaguely, the rule about where the pine tar must stop and he has been warned on three occasions he could recall this season when the umpires noticed how high on his bat the tar appeared.

"They gave me the warnings," Howser said, "and I just get Mickey Cobb (trainer) to put some alcohol to it and clean it up. That's what they should have done this time: given us a warning."

Brett said he applies the pine tar from the trademark downward. "Then I just turn the bats over to our equipment man (Al Zych), he puts them in a trunk and when I need one he gives it to me."

The Associated Press

◆ Umpire Tim McClelland measures the pine tar on the handle of George Brett's bat as New York Yankee manager Billy Martin watches in a July 24, 1983, game at Yankee Stadium. McClelland called Brett out for too much pine tar. The incident has become known as the "Pine Tar Home Run."

Habitually Brett will massage his bat while in the on-deck circle or the batter's box. As with many hitters, he applies extra pine tar above the bat handle so he can rub some fresh onto his hands at any time. He believes that is where the smudges come from that extend into the no-no zone; that, and from rolling around on the ground.

"It should have occurred to somebody that was dirt up high on my bat," Brett said. "It definitely wasn't illegal." ◆

The Rule

The bat handle, for not more than 18 inches from the end, may be covered or treated with any material or substance to improve the grip. Any such material, including pine tar, which extends past the 18-inch limitation, in the umpire's judgement, shall cause the bat to be removed from the game. No such material shall improve the reaction or distance factor of the bat.

42 inch maximum bat size

Trademark

Pine tar

Source: The Rules of Baseball 1983   The Star

July 25, 1983

Too much tar didn't cost Royals in '75

By DALE PHELPS

George Brett was not the first Royals player to be challenged for illegal use of pine tar.

The California Angels protested an 8-7 loss in 11 innings to the Royals in 1975. The Angels accused John Mayberry of the Royals, who hit two home runs in the game, of using pine tar too far up the bat handle. American League President Lee MacPhail

The Associated Press

Lee MacPhail

turned down the Angels' protest, saying he was following the spirit of the rule on the actual hitting surface rather than getting technical about the number of inches of pine tar on the bat.

Although Mayberry was not punished, several players have suffered the consequences of using illegal bats.

In addition to batters, pitchers have been ejected for using illegal equipment — mostly in the form of doctored baseballs.

IT'S A HOMER, BY GEORGE!

◆

From STAFF and WIRE REPORTS

AMERICAN LEAGUE PRESIDENT RESTORES BRETT'S HOMER AGAINST YANKEES

July 28, 1983

Well, the umpires didn't win this one.

American League President Lee MacPhail overruled the umpires today and ordered that George Brett's two-run homer against the New York Yankees last Sunday count, though it was hit with a bat which the umpires said was illegal because of excessive pine tar.

It was the first time in MacPhail's 10-year tenure that he has overruled the umpires.

The Yankees had been declared 4-3 winners over the Royals when the umpires disallowed Brett's home run and recorded it instead as the final out.

Now, the game will be treated as a suspended game and must be completed, if practical. It would be resumed with two outs in the top of the ninth with the Royals leading 5-4. Because the Royals and Yankees are not scheduled to play each other the rest of the season, the game will be completed only if first place is at stake for either team, according to Bob Fishel, assistant to MacPhail.

◆ **The Kansas City Royals announce at a press conference they will appeal the "Pine Tar Home Run" ruling.**

"It could be the 18th (of August)," Fishel said. "It could be the day after the end of the season. It could never be played."

All records, including Brett's home run, will count, however.

Fishel said a decision would be made later on possible disciplinary action against Brett, who bumped an umpire in the uproar that followed the decision nullifying the home run. The plate umpire was Tim McClelland, and the umpire crew chief was Joe Brinkman.

CALL IT A STICKY DEAL

——————— ◆ ———————

By MIKE FISH

BRETT MAKES TRADE TO BRING PINE-TAR BAT HOME
August 10, 1984

So you want to bargain, do you?

Well, George Brett apparently is adept at recognizing a good deal when he sees one.

You may recall Brett negotiated a "lifetime" contract with Royals co-owner Avron Fogelman this spring. Big bucks, right?

All Brett was asked to do was go about his baseball business for the next decade or so. But Fogelman wasn't done dealing. His final demand was for Brett to get his hands on the celebrated pine-tar bat so it could be put on display at Royals Stadium.

That was accomplished recently when New Jersey sports collector Barry Halper graciously returned the bat. Brett had given the bat to Halper, a friend and limited partner in the New York Yankees, after the controversial game last summer at Yankee Stadium.

"Mr. Fogelman mentioned in the negotiations how he would like to have the bat back," Brett said. "It was a friendly statement. I mean, here was a guy who had gone out on the limb for me. The least I could do was go out on a limb and get it back for him."

According to Brett, the bat is in Fogelman's possession.

K.C. Star

Although the umpires are being overruled, it is not the fault of the umpires — rather it is the fault of the official playing rules. The bat definitely had more than 18 inches of pine tar, and yes, Brett will get his bat back." The league had locked up the bat while studying the case.

Shortly after receiving a phone call from Fishel, informing him of the decision, Royals General Manager John Schuerholz said, "I was delighted. I didn't jump up and down but I had hoped that based on the evidence we presented, the AL would rule in our favor."

The Yankees, however, were not delighted.

Fishel quoted Yankees owner George Steinbrenner as saying, "Rules are rules and you guys aren't observing them ... I know you guys are friends of mine, but we're very unhappy. ..."

Schuerholz said the Royals would have to study the schedule to find a time the game possibly could be replayed.

"Off the top," Schuerholz said, "I'd have to say it would have to be completed at the end of the season."

Schuerholz said he thought the decision was based on the spirit of the rules applying to this incident.

The Royals' full statement today:

"It has been our position all along that a clarification of the Official Baseball Rules would support our protest. We are deeply appreciative of the time and thought that MacPhail and the American League gave to this decision. We are also appreciative of the tremendous show of support we have received from our fans all over the country.

"Finally, the Royals are most pleased that the multitude of baseball fans around the world assured that the outcome of classic baseball confrontations will be decided by the players on the field."

The reversal means the Royals gain one-half game in the AL West standings, and the Yankees drop one-half game behind in the AL East. The Royals now trail the Chicago White Sox by two games instead of 2^{1}/$_{2}$.

Schuerholz also said that MacPhail worked with the Playing Rules Committee in reaching his decision. The chairman of the committee is William A. Murray of the commissioner's office.

Schuerholz said that the Royals' protest cited a 1975 ruling in which MacPhail denied a protest lodged by the California Angels over a bat used by the Royals' John Mayberry, who had hit two homers in an 8-7 Kansas City victory. MacPhail ruled at that time that the pine tar had nothing to do with Mayberry's home runs.

Royals pitcher Dan Quisenberry said: "My attitude is too prejudiced. I think every pitch is a strike, and on every play our guy is safe. And every beef, I think we're right. If I was the pitcher (Rich Gossage), I wouldn't want it changed, and I'm not glad to go back to New York, but I am glad to have a chance for another win."

The controversy began Sunday when Brett hit a two-run homer with two outs in the top of the ninth against the Yankees, boosting the Royals into a 5-4 lead.

McClelland was reached in Detroit where he will be an umpire in the Royals' series this weekend against the Detroit Tigers. "It did surprise us," McClelland said. ◆

Brett was playing golf today and was unavailable for comment.

Said MacPhail, reading from a two-page statement in New York:

"It is the position of this office that the umpires' interpretation, while technically defensible, is not in accord with the intent or spirit of the rules and that the rules do not provide that a hitter be called out for excessive use of pine tar.

"It was a very tough decision for me.

"It wasn't me personally asking George," said Fogelman, who also is a collector of baseball memorabilia. "I was representing the Royals in the conversation. We felt the bat should be here."

Brett said Halper was very understanding when Brett told him of his predicament last spring.

For his part, Brett offered Halper the bat he used in hitting three homers off Catfish Hunter during a 1978 playoff game.

"We also don't know just when, but at some time we're going to loan the bat to the Hall of Fame to display." ◆

The Associated Press

◆ **Brett displays the bat used to hit the famous "Pine Tar Home Run."**

Twins haven't overlooked Brett's restroom rampage

By MIKE FISH

The Royals can expect a bill in the near future for the damage that George Brett caused in a Metropolitan Stadium restroom during Friday night's game with the Minnesota Twins.

The only question is who will reimburse the Twins: the all-star third baseman or the Royals? After grounding out with runners on base, Brett went into a restroom behind the dugout and used his bat to break two toilets and a sink. A Twins' spokesman said the fixtures would have to be replaced, although the club will be moving next season to the Metrodome, which is under construction in downtown Minneapolis.

The restroom damage came about two weeks after Brett had struck a United Press International photographer, Tom Gralish, with a crutch. Brett swung the crutch at the photographer May 14, when Brett had injured his right ankle in a game with the Texas Rangers and was leaving Royals Stadium for X-rays at a hospital.

Joe Burke, the Royals' executive vice president and general manager, said: "We'll have to wait and see all the details before determining who's responsible for the expense. This has happened before, and it's not that uncommon. Guys have hit a wall or a trash can with their bats. It's happened in almost every stadium I've been in."

Before Monday night's game with the Seattle Mariners, Brett was visibly outraged that the restroom damage had been reported in *The Kansas City Times*. He implied that he had a right to privacy, just as an individual who might punch a hole in the wall of his home would not see his name in the newspaper.

"I don't think it's anybody's business," Brett said. "It's already written, so why should I discuss it?"

PHOTOGRAPHER HIT BY BRETT'S CRUTCH

◆

From STAFF and WIRE REPORTS

◆ Brett swings a crutch at a UPI photographer as he was about to get on an elevator outside the Royals clubhouse after spraining his ankle in a game with the Texas Rangers.

May 15, 1981

Kansas City third baseman George Brett struck a news photographer in the head with a crutch as Brett was leaving Royals Stadium during Thursday night's game with the Texas Rangers.

Tom Gralish, a photographer for United Press International, was struck above the right eye but was not hurt seriously. Brett was leaving for St. Luke's Hospital with an ankle injury.

Brett, who had been hurt sliding into home plate in the fourth inning, was with teammate Clint Hurdle. They were waiting for the clubhouse elevator.

"Brett stuck out his crutch and hit me with a swipe up and caught my camera on the way down," Gralish said.

"He said, 'Don't you have anything ... better to take pictures of?' I was stunned." ◆

Brett and *Times* reporter scuffle at California hotel

By MIKE McKENZIE

ANAHEIM, Calif. — Mike Fish, who covers the Royals for *The Kansas City Times*, and Royals third baseman George Brett had to be refrained from fighting each other after Monday night's 4-3 Royals victory over the California Angels.

According to several witnesses, no punches landed. Fish was scratched beneath both eyes when he was pinned against a wall by Dean Vogelaar, the Royals' public relations director. Brett was pulled aside by teammates Greg Keatley and Willie Wilson.

The incident occurred about 1:30 a.m. Tuesday in a lobby hallway at the Anaheim Hyatt. Police were summoned, but no arrests were made.

Tempers flared after Brett and Vogelaar made remarks about news stories that Fish had written June 1 and 2. He had reported that Brett had broken up two toilets and a sink in a ballpark restroom in Bloomington, Minn.

Brett had been standing in the hotel hallway with two women friends. Fish walked by the sportswriter Alan Eskew of *The Topeka Capital Journal*; Janis Carr, a reporter formerly with *The Los Angeles Times* who will begin working September 28 for *The Kansas City Star*; and Ms. Carr's sister. Brett said something to Fish related to the Minnesota story. Both agreed that the remark had been made in a joking fashion.

Then Vogelaar joined the group and Ms. Carr entered the conversation.

"I told him, 'Don't you think you put yourself into the limelight as an athlete?' And he pointed his finger in my face," Ms. Carr said. "I don't have to stand for that. I pushed his hand away. Then he pushed my face with his fingertips with some force."

Fish responded. "I said something like, 'You can't do that,' and he swung at me," Fish said.

Brett's version was similar.

"Suddenly, this girl I don't know, and who doesn't know me, starts laying into me about how I should act, and what kind of person I am," Brett said. "The more lip I got, the more excited I got.

"I told the girl, 'That's it. I've had enough,' and I pushed her a little and turned away. Some shouting occurred, things were said, minor actions were taken, then Dean did his job — peacemaker, separating us."

BRETT'S NOTABLE INJURIES

George Brett missed more than 350 games, just over two full seasons, because of injuries ranging from torn knee ligaments to a broken toe. Without the injuries, Brett probably would have added about 300 hits to his career total of 3,154.

1984
Tore medial collateral ligament in left knee toward the end of spring training. Missed first 33 games. Tore left hamstring going from home-run trot to sprint after hitting ball off top of Green Monster at Fenway Park. Missed 23 games. Batted .284 and failed to steal a base for second straight season.

1983
Broke left little toe on door jamb while hurrying to watch Bill Buckner bat. Missed 20 games. Finished with .310 average.

1979
Fractured right thumb while diving for loose ball during off-season charity basketball game. Recovered before season began and batted .329 with career-high 20 triples.

1978
Injured left shoulder in collision at second base; later had bone chip at base of right thumb. Batted .294 with career-high 23 stolen bases.

1986
Right shoulder problems cost him 42 games. Batted .290.

1991
Missed 26 games because of partial tear of medial collateral ligament in right knee. Didn't play in the field for rest of season. Batted a career-low .255.

1987
Missed more than 40 games because of rib-cage injury he suffered while swinging at pitch. Also suffered partial tear of medial collateral ligament in right knee. Missed All-Star Game because of sore right shoulder. Batted .290.

1980
Missed 44 games because of heel, ankle and thumb injuries. Still won American League batting title with .390 average.

1989
Missed 35 games because of torn medial collateral ligament in right knee. Batted .282.

Thumb

Shoulder

Rib cage

Hamstring

Medial collateral ligament (knee)

Heel

Ankle

Toe

DAVE EAMES/The Star

◆ Brett hugs Frank White after the final out of game three of the American League Championship Series against the Toronto Blue Jays. The Royals defeated the Blue Jays 6-5 and Brett matched the league championship record with four runs.

BRETT SNATCHES ROYALS FROM BRINK

◆

By TRACY RINGOLSBY

LOSS STRING IS ENDED DRAMATICALLY

October 12, 1985

George Brett refused to let the Royals' playoff hopes die Friday night.

The Royals came off the critical list with a 6-5 victory over Toronto, ending a 10-game post-season losing streak that included the first two games of this AL playoff series, in Toronto. Kansas City will try to tie the series at two games apiece at 7:15 tonight at Royals Stadium.

Steve Farr got the victory. He faced the minimum of 13 batters in 4⅓ innings of shutout relief, although he did give up two singles.

Steve Balboni got the game-winning RBI. With the score tied 5-5 and two outs in the bottom of the eighth, he blooped a single into center field, scoring Brett from third base with Balboni's first hit in 12 at-bats this series.

But the night belonged to Brett.

◆ **At the plate:** He homered twice — a bases-empty shot in the first inning that put the Royals up 1-0 and a two-run shot in the sixth that tied the game 5-5; he doubled and scored, giving the Royals a 2-0 lead in the fourth; and he singled and scored the game-winner in the eighth.

◆ **In the field:** With the Royals holding a 1-0 lead in the third inning, one out and Damaso Garcia on third, Brett backhanded a ground ball by Lloyd Moseby down the line behind third base and made an off-balance throw to catcher Jim Sundberg, who tagged Garcia out.

◆ And in the hearts of the 40,224 fans at Royals Stadium, and his teammates.

◆ **Brett hits his second homer of the game against the Toronto Blue Jays in game three of the 1985 American League Championship Series in Kansas City on October 11, 1985.**

Jim McTaggart

The fans afforded him four standing ovations. His teammates mobbed Brett at third base after he caught Moseby's pop-up in foul territory for the final out in Manager Dick Howser's first victory after 11 post-season losses.

"The difference between us and everyone else is George Brett," Royals reserve Dane Iorg said. "Willie Wilson does a good job. Steve Balboni gets the game-winning RBI, and Steve Farr does a great job. But George ... You keep thinking he's done everything and can't do it again. He doesn't rise to an occasion. He's always in a class by himself."

He came through when the Royals needed him in the final week of the season. They won five of six games on the way to clinching the AL West title, and Brett homered in each of the games, including the three of four the Royals won from the AL West challenger California.

And then on Friday night, when another loss would have pretty well buried the Royals in this best-of-seven series, he came through

with four hits, four runs scored and three RBI in four at-bats. He was thrown 11 pitches and had 11 total bases.

The Blue Jays tried to stop him. Starting pitcher Doyle Alexander threw him a change-up in the first inning, and Brett hit it for a home run. Alexander threw him a slider in the fourth inning, and Brett led off by hitting a double off the right-field wall. And he threw him a fastball in the sixth, after Wilson led off with a single. Brett drove it out of the park to left field.

Even in the eighth, when he admitted he had his worst swing of the game, he was able to ground a change-up from reliever and loser Jim Clancy into right field for a single.

"If he's not the best hitter in baseball, I don't know who is," Blue Jays catcher Ernie Whitt said. "You can't pitch him one way. When he gets in a hot streak, you can't get him out. I might just start telling him what is coming. I'll tell him, 'Fastball down the middle.' Maybe he will pop it up."

There was no maybe about the impact Brett had on the Royals in this game. Things had looked bleak when the Blue Jays rallied from a 2-0 deficit. They hit Royals starter Bret Saberhagen hard — literally and figuratively — with a five-run rally in the fifth that included two-run home runs by Jesse Barfield and Rance Mulliniks in a playoff-record-tying seven hits.

"You have to use a whole thesaurus to describe him," Quisenberry said of Brett. "It's like Jamie Quirk said in the bullpen after George's second home run: 'We're in the driver's seat now. George has one more at-bat.'" ◆

◆ Brett acknowledges the fans after hitting his second home run in game three of the playoffs against the Toronto Blue Jays.

BRETT PUTS HIS STAMP ON SERIES

◆

By JOE McGUFF

October 12, 1985

If you weren't there Friday night for game three of the American League Championship Series, you should have been. If you were there, you saw a performance that will become a part of baseball's post-season lore along with Don Larsen's perfect World Series game, Babe Ruth's called-shot home run and Reggie Jackson's three home runs in the sixth game of the 1977 Series.

There are rare and wonderful moments when a great athlete throws aside the restraints that his humanity places on him and plays at a level that fills us with joy and awe. Friday night was one of those occasions.

Perhaps never has one player so dominated a big game as George Brett did. The Royals were gasping for life in their playoff series with Toronto. They had lost the first two games and were at risk of losing their 11th straight game in post-season play.

Brett hit a home run over the right-field fence in the first inning. He hit a double that was two feet from the top of the right-field wall in the fourth. He hit a home run to deep left-center in the sixth. In the eighth, he singled and scored the winning run.

He also executed a defensive play in the genre of Brooks Robinson's vacuum-cleaner performance in the 1970 World Series. In the third inning Brett made a backhand stop of Lloyd Moseby's sharply hit ball down the third-base line, leaped and threw across his body to retire the fleet Damaso Garcia, who attempted to score from third.

Saturday night the Royals lost to the Blue Jays 3-1 and trail in the series three games to one, but in years to come the series between the Royals and the Blue Jays will be remembered not so much for who won or lost, but because of what Brett did in the third game. It was a performance that makes the spirit soar and creates the sort of excitement that is renewable every time the sights and sounds of this night come to mind.

Big games in post-season play are nothing new for Brett, but the totality of his per-

◆ **Doyle Alexander**

Cliff Schiappa

Royals 6, Blue Jays 5

TORONTO	ab	r	h	bi	KANSAS CITY	ab	r	h	bi
Garcia 2b	5	1	2	0	L. Smith lf	4	0	1	0
Moseby cf	4	1	1	1	L. Jones lf	0	0	0	0
Mulliniks 3b	4	1	1	2	Wilson cf	4	1	2	0
Upshaw 1b	4	0	1	0	Brett 3b	4	4	4	3
Oliver dh	2	0	1	0	McRae dh	3	0	1	0
C. Johnson dh	2	0	1	0	White 2b	3	0	0	1
G. Bell lf	4	0	3	0	Sheridan rf	3	0	0	0
Whitt c	3	1	1	0	Balboni 1b	4	0	1	1
Barfield rf	4	1	1	2	Sundberg c	4	1	1	1
Fernandez ss	4	0	1	0	Biancalana ss	1	0	0	0
					D. Iorg ph	1	0	0	0
					Concepcion ss	1	0	0	0
Totals	36	5	13	5	**Totals**	32	6	10	6

Toronto	000	050	000 — 5
Kansas City	100	112	01x — 6

E: Upshaw, L.Smith. DP: Kansas City 3. LOB: Toronto 6, Kansas City 5. 2B: Garcia 2, Brett, Upshaw, McRae. HR: Brett 2 (2), Barfield (1), Mulliniks (1), Sundberg (1). S:McRae. SF: White. GAME WINNING RBI: Balboni (1).

Toronto	IP	H	R	ER	BB	SO
a- Alexander	5	7	5	5	0	3
Lamp	2	1	0	0	0	2
Clancy (L, 0-1)	1	2	1	1	1	0
Kansas City						
Saberhagen	4⅓	9	5	5	1	4
Black	⅓	2	0	0	1	0
Farr (W, 1-0)	4⅓	2	0	0	0	3

a-Pitched to three batters in sixth

Umpires: HP, Evans; 1B, Hendry; 2B, Voltaggio; 3B, Cousins; LF, Phillips; RF, Ford.. Time: 2:51. Announced attendance: 40,224.

formance in such a desperate situation goes beyond anything he has done before.

"We are awed by his talents," said Jamie Quirk, the Royals' reserve catcher and one of Brett's close friends. "When I came up to him after the game, I told him, 'I don't know what to say. You are unbelievable.' I'm glad that when I'm 50 I'll be able to say I played with George Brett."

John Wathan, shaking his head in wonderment, recalled a scene on the bench in the sixth.

"When George came up," Wathan related, "Jamie said, 'If he hits a home run, I'll take my clothes off and run on the field naked.' Jamie didn't do it, but I had his top two buttons off. Every time there is a big game, George is phenomenal."

Manager Dick Howser talked about the difficulty of pitching to Brett, who hits to all fields and has no obvious weakness.

"One club had five scouts who all happened to meet here to look at George," Howser said. "And they all disagreed on how to pitch to him."

Howser refused to identify the club, but another source with the Royals said Toronto had five scouts following the club.

"When I managed the Yankees and we played the Royals in 1980, nobody could really agree on how to pitch to George," Howser continued. "We had Bob Nieman, Birdie Tebbetts, Jerry Walker and Harry Craft scouting the Royals that year. One was a catcher, two were outfielders and one was a pitcher, and no one could agree. That is the ultimate compliment."

Why is Brett so good in big games?

"I think he enjoys having people rely on him," Quick said. "He likes to carry the team. His concentration is phenomenal. He has greater concentration than anyone I've ever played with."

The most poignant moment Friday night came when Brett was asked about the time earlier in the season when he came out of a slump after reviewing a video tape he made with the late Charley Lau, who was the Royals' hitting instructor in the early years of Brett's career.

"I knew what was on the tape," Brett said, "but I wanted to see his smiling face and remind myself of all the time we spent together. The good times and the bad. Today I hope there's a smile on his face if they have color television in heaven."

As Brett left the clubhouse Friday night he paused at the door of Howser's office.

"Nice managing, Skip." ◆

Dan Siefert

◆ Brett talks to fans in Kansas City before the start of game one of the 1985 World Series against the St. Louis Cardinals.

Dan Siefert

◆ Brett tags Willie McGee during game one of the 1985 World Series.

◆ A glum Royals' bench watches as Kansas City loses game one, 3-1, to the St. Louis Cardinals.

◆ Brett (left) and Bret Saberhagen confer near the mound during game three of the 1985 World Series in St. Louis.

♦ Brett prepares to tag Willie McGee during game four.

♦ Brett, after striking out for the second time against Cardinals pitcher John Tudor in game five of the 1985 World Series.

♦ Brett injured his eye in game five, when he slid into the Royals dugout chasing a fly ball. Batting instructor Lee May caught Brett and prevented serious injury.

1985
WORLD SERIES

◆

GAME 1 - Oct. 19
St. Louis 3, Kansas City 1

GAME 2 - Oct. 20
St. Louis 4, Kansas City 2

GAME 3 - Oct. 22
Kansas City 6, St. Louis 1

GAME 4 - Oct. 23
St. Louis 3, Kansas City 0

GAME 5 - Oct. 24
Kansas City 6, St. Louis 1

GAME 6 - Oct. 26
Kansas City 2, St. Louis 1

GAME 7 - Oct. 27
Kansas City 11, St. Louis 0

Jim McTaggart

◆ Brett at bat in game six. The Royals won the game 2-1, scoring both their runs in the ninth inning.

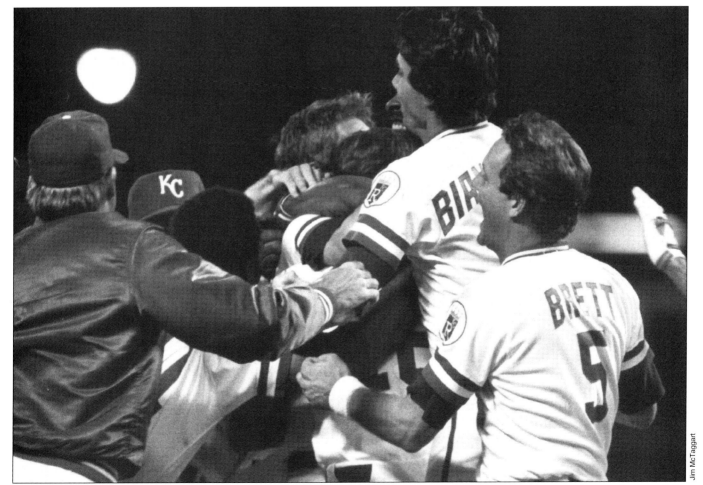

Jim McTaggart

◆ Brett and other Royals mob Dane Iorg after Iorg's single in the bottom of the ninth drove in the winning run as the Royals evened the Series at 3-3.

◆ **Pitcher Joe Beckwith douses Brett with champagne after the Royals win the 1985 World Series against the St. Louis Cardinals.**

AFTER YEARS OF WAITING, SCHOOL IS FINALLY OUT FOR ROYALS' CLASS OF '73

◆

By SID BORDMAN

October 28, 1985

In the ninth inning Sunday night Hal McRae stepped up his pacing of the Royals' dugout, leading cheers for his club.

At the same time George Brett and Frank White were on the field, helping put the finishing touches on the 11-0 rout that gave Kansas City its first World Series championship.

The Class of '73 had reached the highest mountain.

"Great, unbelievable," said McRae, who was legislated out of the mainstream of the World Series because of the exclusion of the designated hitter this year.

Twelve years ago McRae (in a trade from Cincinnati), White and Brett (both from the Royals' minor-league system), joined the Royals for the first time.

"I was excited," McRae said. "It's a good feeling that we could win without me playing. Everybody made such a big deal of no DH. I didn't want that to be a negative factor. Sure, I felt disappointed, but I would never admit it. We didn't want to feel sorry for ourselves. Frankly, I don't think I'd feel any better than I do now if I had played."

White, the great-fielding second baseman who was elevated to the No. 4 position in the Royals' hitting order with McRae out, said he didn't want to go into the past, a la 1973.

"But I thought it would eventually happen," White said. "I thought we would win it in 1980 (the Royals lost to Philadelphia in the World Series). We've made changes, and that did it. George, Mac — and don't forget Duke Wathan — we've done a lot, and we have to be proud. This feels better than anything we ever did, and it will feel better tomorrow.

"Somebody asked if being a hometown player made it extra special. Right now, I can't say. Maybe tomorrow I'll have something good to say."

Brett, the slugging third baseman who had four hits in the finale, agreed with White and McRae.

◆ **A drenched, delirious Brett celebrates the world championship.**

"This is the best thing that has happened to Frank and me," he said. "Frank and I started together in 1971 in the instructional league. Mac came over from a big-league club and had been in a World Series. We've shared a lot, those defeats against New York in the playoffs and against Philadelphia.

"Now we know how to do it. Imagine, it took us 176 games to have a laugher. I'm going to have a beer. I hate champagne."

McRae said the 1973 Royals were a good team.

"We were only a few players away because we were strong down the middle with Cookie Rojas, Freddie Patek and Amos Otis," he said. "And don't forget we had John Mayberry."

McRae was overflowing with confidence before the game, which triggered the flowing and pouring of champagne on everybody in sight.

"I said we could beat them all alone," McRae said.

"They had such a buildup coming in. After the first night I was certain we could beat them. They weren't swinging the bats well, and Jack Clark was the only one with power. Our pitchers did a heck of a job of jamming their hitters.

"Because we came back: That's why this is the biggest thrill of all my years in the big leagues (16). We were down, but we didn't get tight. When we were down, we played extremely well. This is a big thing for all of us, especially Frank, George and me. We have a good mixture of vets and young guys."

John Schuerholz, general manager of the Royals, focused on White, Brett and McRae.

"The three are cornerstones," he said. "They brought a lot of quality, provided a lot of leadership. Because of both, the three are something special."

The Class of '73. A night to remember. ◆

◆ Brett won his only Gold Glove for his sterling defensive play in the 1985 season.

GOLD GLOVE SHOWS BRETT SCOOPED UP SOME BELIEVERS

◆

By Tracy Ringolsby

December 3, 1985

George Brett says he is going to put the Gold Glove he was awarded Tuesday next to the bat from the Pine Tar Game in his family's Manhattan Beach, Calif., restaurant.

"We'll call it the Ripley's Believe It or Not Department," Brett said.

Two years after Brett approached the Royals about moving from third base to another position, American League managers and coaches voted him the best-fielding third baseman in the league in 1985.

Brett was selected on 19 of the 77 ballots for the award given annually by *The Sporting News*. Brook Jacoby of Cleveland was second with 16 votes, Wade Boggs of Boston and Jim Presley of Seattle tied for third with 10 votes, and Doug DeCinces of California had nine.

Certainly, the trade of Buddy Bell from Texas to Cincinnati in the middle of the 1985 season played a part in Brett's selection. Bell won the award for third baseman the six previous seasons.

"He definitely had a good reputation, the best in the American League," Brett said of Bell. "With players like Buddy and Graig Nettles (now with San Diego), they are known as defensive players who can hit a little. I was an offensive player who could field a little.

"When people talked about me, they always talked hitting. After this season, I can be counted as a complete baseball player, not just an offensive player."

◆ **Brett stopped Tommy Herr's hard grounder in game two of the World Series against the Cardinals and threw to first for the out.**

Brett said he thought his efforts in 1985 were his all-time best. He hit .335, had 112 runs batted in and hit a career-high 30 home runs. Defensively, Brett led AL third basemen in assists with 339 and double plays with 33.

Brett made only 15 errors in 461 chances, and his .967 fielding percentage ranked second among AL third basemen who appeared in at least 100 games. Rance Mulliniks, who platooned at third base in Toronto, had a .971 percentage.

"Two months ago, a friend told me not to get my hopes up about winning the MVP, but he said I had a good chance to win the Gold Glove," Brett said. "I just laughed. With third basemen like Boggs and DeCinces, there's still some tough competition, but none of us had a name for ourselves defensively like Buddy.

"I didn't want to get my hopes up, but I thought I had a good enough year to deserve it.

I thought I had a good enough year for the MVP, too, but ... ."

Brett finished second in AL MVP voting to Don Mattingly of the New York Yankees. Both Brett, who won AL MVP honors in 1980, and Mattingly, a first baseman, were Gold Glove winners.

"This is something I never thought I could win," Brett said. "I didn't have much confidence in my ability to play the position (two years ago when he asked to move to first base or left field).

"This year, I came to spring training in great shape, performed well during the exhibition season, and my confidence was at an all-time high."

Brett appeared in 155 games, his most since 1976. And, Brett said, most importantly, the Royals won their first world championship.

"All of this couldn't have come at a better time," Brett said, referring to a disappointing 1984 in which he was bothered by injuries from spring training through the end of the season. "People were coming around during spring training with polls about different awards. One guy asked me who I thought would be the comeback player of the year. I told him, 'I will be. I'm going to have a year you've never seen before.'"

Brett hit for a higher average in 1980, when he batted .390, the best mark in the major leagues since Ted Williams hit .406 for Boston in 1941. He also drove in a career-high 118 runs that year. But he played in only 117 games. ◆

THE ROAD TO COOPERSTOWN
1986 ◆ 1993

It's not enough to be baseball's best player for a season or two. Not to get to Cooperstown.

A pivotal part in the playoffs or a starring role in the World Series is not enough either. Not to get to Cooperstown.

To join baseball's Hall of Fame in Cooperstown, N.Y., a player needs a career of standout seasons, a pile of memorable performances and maybe a couple of accomplishments no one else can match.

After the Royals won the World Series in 1985, George Brett had convinced Kansas City's fans he belonged in the Hall of Fame. As his career wound down to the day he announced his retirement, Brett piled up enough statistics to convince even the toughest critic.

He added a third batting title, becoming the first player in major-league history to win titles in three different decades. He steadily climbed baseball's career lists, reaching fifth in doubles and leaving only Hall of Fame players ahead of him in most major hitting statistics.

Most memorable was his 3,000th hit, making him the 18th player in history to reach that milestone. It came in a performance Royals fans have come to consider vintage Brett: four hits in a game Brett wasn't even certain he would start because of a shoulder injury.

After reaching 3,000 hits late in the 1992 season, Brett wavered a little before deciding to play again in 1993. Although he never again finished a season batting .300 after his 1990 batting title, Brett still managed to add a couple of milestones in his last season: his 300th home run and his 200th stolen base.

His last major-league swing, naturally, was a hit: No. 3,154.

Even better, the Royals beat the Texas Rangers 4-1.

"Good way to end a career," Brett said. ◆

◆ **Brett strokes his 3,000th hit September 30, 1992, off California Angels pitcher Tim Fortugno at Anaheim.**

BRETT'S SWITCH MIGHT NOT BE TEMPORARY

◆

By DENNIS DODD

June 28, 1987

The first baseman's glove is courtesy of Kevin Seitzer. The pickoff throws come from each member of the Royals' pitching staff in drills. Coach Jim Schaffer hits an endless summer of ground balls.

George Brett is relearning first base.

Manager Billy Gardner made the announcement Friday that Brett is the Royals' regular first baseman for now, switching from third base. The move shouldn't be regarded as a typical move to first by an aging veteran. First base won't be any rocking chair job for Brett, who has played only 25 games at first, counting Saturday's start against the Seattle Mariners.

The switch was made for a variety of reasons that came together Friday when left-handed Jim Eisenreich started his first game for the Royals, replacing Brett as the designated

hitter. Brett had played DH for 13 games following his return from the disabled list.

Brett didn't return to his usual position because Seitzer has won the third-base job with his defense and his bat (.300). First base was open because Steve Balboni has been inconsistent at first and at the plate. Balboni will share the right-handed designated hitter duties with Juan Beniquez.

"They've been talking about putting me at first for years," Brett said. "They've got a guy (Seitzer) who can play third base now, so this might be the logical time to do it."

The key in the move may be Seitzer's defense. Never known as a defensive whiz in the minors, Seitzer has shown a glove to match his bat. And with Brett on the disabled list twice this season, Seitzer has had a chance to stick at third after playing outfield, first and third in less than a season with the Royals.

Balboni, who is batting .209, now is strictly a DH. Beniquez started Saturday against left-handed Lee Guetterman of Seattle. "I'm shocked myself," Seitzer said of his defense. "I always felt I was capable of playing good defense, but I never showed it. I was kind of shaky coming up through the organization. Since he (Brett) was hurt, I put a lot of extra time in it, taking ground balls every day.

"It's going to take (Brett) a while to adjust. The first throw I made to him (in infield drills) went 10 feet over his head. I was looking for Bonesy (Balboni). Throwing to him was like throwing to the side of a barn. Now I just aim for the dirt."

Brett, a virtual rookie with the glove at first, took a glove out of Seitzer's locker before Friday's game because none of Brett's suited him. Brett's first base career started Friday when he made five put-outs without incident.

"You see a lot of third basemen at a certain age they kind of move to first," Brett said. "This is a lot different. You're in the game a lot more. I noticed it a lot yesterday (Friday) when a guy was at first base and I was holding him on. You can't take your eye off the pitcher. The pitcher can turn and throw the ball to you at any time. If I'm looking at the scoreboard, which I might be doing when I'm playing at third, or if I'm looking in the stands or talking to the coach then I can get drilled. You've got to be in the game at all times."

It's possible Brett will become more durable at first base, but Gardner argues against it. At 34, Brett wants to become hot on the opposite corner.

"I need a lot of work over there," Brett said. "It's not something that's going to come naturally. It's different. It's hard to explain. Playing at first base keeps you in the game. Not just pickoff throws. Everything." ◆

◆ **Brett stretches for a wild throw on a pickoff attempt at first base.**

Joe Ledford

BRETT TO STAY AT DH

◆

By JACK ETKIN

HOPE IS THAT STAYING OFF FIELD WILL REDUCE INJURIES

June 8, 1991

Designated hitter is no longer a way station for George Brett, a place where his bat can thrive until his legs are fit enough for him to return to first base.

He will serve primarily as the Royals' full-time DH, which has been his role for 14 games since returning from the disabled list May 24. Because of Brett's situation, Jim Eisenreich took his second lesson at first base with infield coach Bob Schaefer before batting practice began Friday.

The idea of becoming a full-time DH was Brett's, not that of Manager Hal McRae.

"You don't come in making a major move with the franchise player," McRae said.

Brett missed 26 games because of a torn ligament in his right knee after he slipped leaving the batter's box April 22 in Cleveland. He now wears a brace on that knee and an elastic sleeve on his left one.

"I'm 38 years old, and I've had five knee injuries," Brett said. "I want to play. I don't like being on the disabled list. I think if I go out there, being in this big old brace ... I'm in this big old brace for a reason.

"How many times can you do it and keep coming back? For me, I think it's the best thing to stay off the field as much as possible. I think for the team it's the best thing for me to be in the lineup as much as possible."

Brett served as the Royals' DH for 32 games last year, 17 in 1989, 33 in 1988 and 21 in 1987.

Since returning to the Royals' lineup, Brett has gone 16 for 49 (.327) and raised his average to .250. McRae turned the DH role into a successful career and will be there to guide Brett, if need be, through whatever

◆ A partially torn medial collateral ligament in his right knee, suffered in the 12th game of the 1991 season, required Brett to wear a bulky brace. The injury turned Brett into a full-time designated hitter.

Joe Ledford

mental pitfalls he encounters from leaving the field.

"I haven't had a problem with it yet," Brett said. "It's always been on a short-term basis, a day game after a night game. I sit in the dugout and, five hitters before it's my turn to hit, run sprints in the runway and stretch.

"You've got to stay in the game. I think that's the main thing. I've got to stay in the flow of it."

Brett began his career with the Royals at third base and played there through the outset of the 1987 season. After tearing a ligament in his right knee on May 15, Brett served as the DH upon returning and then took over at first base June 26, 1987.

Eisenreich last played first base his junior year in high school. With right fielder Danny Tartabull out because of a hand

injury until at least Tuesday, Eisenreich is back in the outfield.

McRae said he ultimately would like Eisenreich or Carmelo Martinez to log most of the time at first base and bat fifth.

"I'm really looking for production," McRae said. "Whoever can give that to us is the guy who can play every day."

Eisenreich said first base now presents to him "stuff I've probably forgotten," but a comfort level should result.

"I'd like to play the outfield," Eisenreich said, "but it really doesn't matter that much. I've always thought first base would be a place you could play a long time and save wear and tear on the legs and the arm, especially. You don't have to make too many throws as a first baseman, and that's great for me because my arm's not the greatest." ◆

HIT MAKES HISTORY FOR BRETT

◆

By JACK ETKIN

◆ George Brett's classic swing is captured in a multiple exposure.

1-FOR-1 GAME GIVES ROYALS FIRST BASEMAN HIS THIRD BATTING CROWN

October 4, 1990

A season that began so ruinously for George Brett that he drifted into self-doubt ended in triumph Wednesday, when he won his third American League batting title and made baseball history.

With a sacrifice fly and a single in the Royals' 5-2 defeat in Cleveland, officially a one-for-one game, Brett finished with a .329 average. He and Rickey Henderson of the Oakland Athletics dueled in the waning days of the season, jockeying for position by playing intermittently. Henderson went one for three Wednesday and ended with an average of .325.

Brett led the league in hitting in 1976 and 1980 and became the first player to ever win a batting championship in three different decades. To do so, he made a mountainous climb that left him somewhat stunned.

"It's absolutely crazy to be so bad for so long and turn it around and be written off and come back the way I did," Brett said at Kansas City International Airport after the Royals' charter landed. "Never in my wildest dreams did I ever think I'd win a batting title this year. I thought my career was over four or five months ago."

On May 7, Brett was batting .200. Eight days later, he turned 37 and was still burdened with a .234 average. As late as June 30, Brett's average was a modest .256.

When play resumed July 11 after the All-Star break, Brett had a three-hit game at Baltimore and the start of a sizzling stretch.

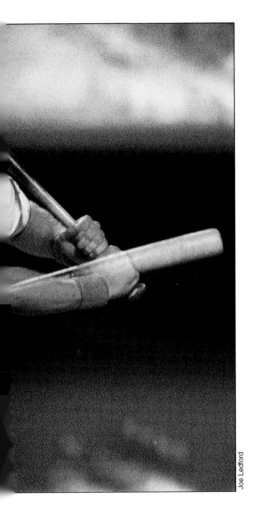

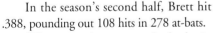
♦ **Brett rests during batting practice.**

In the season's second half, Brett hit .388, pounding out 108 hits in 278 at-bats.

"There was just so much doubt in myself early on in the season," Brett said. "I really doubted my ability. I don't anymore."

Brett's quest for the title became the focal point as the Royals wound down a disappointing season. They were sixth in the AL West, their lowest finish since they began play in 1969, and Brett's duel with Henderson and Texas' Rafael Palmeiro took center stage.

After scoring five points to .332 on September 22 with a four-for-four game at Royals Stadium against California, Brett took a

nine-point lead over Palmeiro, who went into the last game of the season out of the race at .319 and a 10-point bulge over Henderson. Brett was then able to strategically approach the batting race.

He did not play Friday or Saturday in Anaheim, Calif., or Tuesday in Cleveland. Brett also used a last tactic to preserve his lead Wednesday. He entered the game as a pinch hitter in the fifth inning and hit a sacrifice fly. In his one official plate appearance, Brett singled, vindicating the plotting in his sparring with Henderson.

"I talked to a lot of people," Brett said. "I talked to not only my teammates; I talked to other players, other managers, other coaches, scouts. 'What would you do if you were me?' And 99 percent of them said, 'Sit. Make him catch you. You've come too far for you to lose it. You've got to make them win it.'

"If I went 0 for 3 or 0 for 4, Ricky would've sat and made me catch him. We had no place to go. The Oakland A's had no place to go; their season was over. When division championships are settled, then it's time to become an individual."

Henderson left the A's game Wednesday after ending the fourth inning by hitting into a force play. Since the Royals and Indians already had concluded their game when the A's took the field, Henderson knew he needed to go three for three, four for four or four for five to pass Brett.

"I really had no say about what Brett did," Henderson told the *Oakland Tribune.*

"As a great ballplayer, I respect him, but I really thought he should've played in California.

"I take my hat off to him. He's a great ballplayer. I guess I feel he did it a little differently than I thought a good ballplayer would."

Brett's .329 average is the lowest to lead the AL since Rod Carew of the Minnesota Twins hit .318 in 1972. That was an inconsequential statistic to Joe Swarts Jr. of North Kansas City, who came to KCI for Brett's return.

A parts driver for Northtowne Lincoln-Mercury, Swarts, 41, unearthed a "George Brett for President" bumper sticker and put it above his work station earlier this summer when Brett began to surge. Those bumper stickers were the rage 10 years ago, after Brett cruised to his second batting titled with a .390 average.

Swarts wasn't here that summer. He spent 14 years in the Army, missing all of the Royals' glory years, and came back to Kansas City at the end of 1987. He took advantage of his first chance to "participate in anything significant the Royals have had," by showing up with his political remnant to honor Brett.

"I'm going to save this and never going to use it," Swarts said. "When he gets in the Hall of Fame, my daughter's going to have it.

"I might get lucky, and George might autograph it for us. I've never tried for an autograph before." ♦

3,000, BY GEORGE!

◆

By DICK KAEGEL

BRETT'S HIT PARADE REACHES MILESTONE

October 1, 1992

ANAHEIM, Calif. — Leave it to George Brett to do the improbable. He always has.

George Brett, after missing two games with a shoulder injury, banged out four hits Wednesday night and reached the historic 3,000 mark.

Brett, the heart and soul of the Royals, became only the 18th player to achieve 3,000 hits.

The milestone hit came in the seventh inning, a one-hop single that rocketed over California Angels second baseman Ken Oberkfell.

Brett couldn't really define his emotions minutes after the game.

"It's really hard to say. My mind's going too fast right now. If I had a beer in my hand, I'd probably be able to do it very easily.

"It happened so quick, I really didn't have time to prepare myself for it. ... But I'm relieved, very relieved."

Brett said the most he wanted out of this game was one hit. "It's such a shock. I came in here needing four hits and I didn't know if I'd take one swing and my season could be over," he said.

"It happened so fast. It was the farthest thing from my mind to get four hits tonight."

Brett wasted no time after getting three hits, a double and two singles off Julio Valera, in his first three at-bats. He drilled the first pitch from Angels left-hander Tim Fortugno, and Oberkfell had no chance to make a play.

Brett was hugged by Royals first-base coach Lynn Jones and shook hands with

◆ Brett sighs with relief as he rounds first base after getting the 3,000th hit of his career.

Joe Ledford

Angels first baseman Gary Gaetti. His Royals teammates poured onto the field and swarmed around him. Some players carried cameras.

Then Brett headed toward the dugout, raising his hands to the cheering crowd. He returned to first base followed by a bank of photographers. Then after an out, perhaps distracted by the moment, Brett was picked off first base by Fortugno.

"I was right in the middle of a conversation with Gaetti and he picked me off," Brett said, laughing.

Brett batted a fifth time in the ninth and again reached base, but this time on an error by Oberkfell. He was replaced by a pinch runner, Gary Thurman.

Typically, Brett's hits were significant in the Royals' 4-0 victory. He scored after a first-inning double, and his third-inning single helped score a run in the third. No. 2,999 was a single to center in the fifth.

"I was sure I could play if I didn't swing any harder than I swung tonight, and I swung very easy tonight," he said.

When Brett arrived in California, his shoulder injury cast an air of uncertainty over reaching 3,000.

The strained left shoulder suffered in Sunday's game in Minnesota caused him to skip the first two games here. Those were the first games that Brett, often hurt throughout his career, had missed this season because of an injury.

After taking batting practice here Monday night, Brett decided to take himself out of the lineup. There was just too much pain, and Lewis Yocum, team physician for the Angels, warned that further injury could end the season for Brett.

Tests at the Kerlan-Jobe Orthopedic Clinic in Inglewood, Calif., Tuesday revealed no tear in his shoulder muscles. He was given a cortisone shot to reduce pain and inflammation but was still unable to play that night.

The drama and apprehension continued before Wednesday night's game.

A cluster of news media watched as Brett hit balls off a batting tee in the tunnel next to the Royals' dugout. After stroking more than 50 balls into a net, Brett pronounced his shoulder ready.

After watching Brett hit off the tee, Royals batting coach Adrian Garrett said: "He didn't swing hard, but he's nice and smooth. I think it'll work for him."

And it did. ◆

◆ Brett gathers the cheers of the fans at Anaheim Stadium into his arms after getting the 3,000th hit of his career.

BRETT BASH ONE FOR FAMILY, FRIENDS TO REMEMBER

◆

By GIB TWYMAN

October 10, 1992

ANAHEIM, Calif. — The celebration in Suite 307 at the Doubletree Hotel was rolling along righteously now.

George Brett's recently aching shoulder had received maybe one pat for each of his 3,000 hits.

The music of "The Hallelujah Chorus" and "The Natural" played at the park during Brett's at bats Wednesday night still seemed to hang in the room.

Suddenly, George's brother, Kemer — Ken Brett — asked for silence. He stood on a chair and offered a toast to the 18th member of the 3,000-hit club, but more important, the sixth member of his family.

"Here's to George," Kemer said. "This is a special occasion with all his friends here and his brothers here and, you wish, his dad here.

"Jack's here," several voices said in unison. "He is here."

"Hear, hear," said George, raising a glass.

Kicking back had begun in earnest for Brett. The room was full of family and teammates and friends as thick as blood.

There were wife Leslie and mom Ethel Johnson and her husband, Virgil. There was Team Brett from Kansas City — Joanie Frey, Ed Molotsky, R.J. Samuels, Dave and Scottie Broderick and Judy Ireland. There were the El Segundo Beach Bum Boys — Bobby Lowe, Dave Brubaker, John Altamura and the Obradovich brothers, Jim and Steve.

And their dad, Bob Obradovich. "He's been like a second father to me," Brett said.

"Most of the people in that room, I've known all my life. It's a great feeling to share this with them."

They are the people with whom Brett feels most natural. So comfortable that when

they raised a glass of bubbly to toast him, he hoisted a Bud Light.

"I hate champagne," said the man of many perfectly good years.

And the bouquet of this most excellent label, 1992, lingered as Brett came to the park Thursday.

He got a baseball signed by another warhorse, Bert Blyleven of the Angels, teasing him about a couple of scratch hits Wednesday night.

Especially one on a hanging curveball.

"I'd have hit that one out of the park," Blyleven wrote. ◆

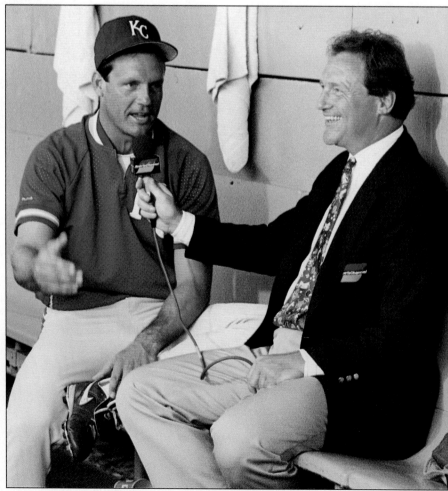

◆ Brett is interviewed by his brother Ken Brett before the game on September 30, 1992. Later that night Brett went 4-for-4 and collected his 3,000th hit.

♦ Five-month-old Jackson Brett sits at his dad's and mom's feet during introductions at the annual Royals Father-Kids game on August 10, 1993.

SUN JUST IN TIME FOR WEDDING

♦

BRETT AND BRIDE HAD HECTIC WEEK AFTER EXCHANGING VOWS

February 27, 1992

BASEBALL CITY, Fla. — George Brett and Leslie Davenport have been married for a dozen days now.

"And they said it wouldn't last," Brett said, grinning.

Brett, one of the game's most eligible bachelors, kept details of his February 15 wedding in California secret to avoid the glare of publicity. It was a small affair.

"Her immediate family, my immediate family," Brett said. "It comes out to 29. We had it at my brother Bobby's house in Manhattan Beach.

"It'd rained for four days and at 3:30 the sun came out. We got married inside the house, but it made it a lot prettier with the sunset in the background because he's got a big house on the ocean there. The best man was my nephew, Kemer's kid Casey, 4½, and the maid of honor was his twin sister, Sheridan."

"Kemer" is brother Ken Brett, a former Royals pitcher. ♦

♦ George Brett and his wife Leslie introduce Jackson Brett.

BRETTS ARE PARENTS

♦

March 8, 1993

BASEBALL CITY, Fla. — Oh baby! It's a boy.

Kansas City's most anticipated birth of the year took place Monday morning at 7:20 when Leslie Brett delivered Jackson Richard at St. Luke's Hospital.

Jackson Richard Brett, 8 pounds, 9 ounces, is 20½ inches long and has thick, dark hair.

Father George and Leslie, and their first-born, are resting comfortably.

"It was unbelievable," George said by phone from the hospital. "The most amazing thing was first seeing it, and knowing you have a baby, and then seeing it after a shampoo and everything. Then it all hits you. It's a baby." ♦

BRETT SAYS TEAM WANTS HIM TO QUIT

◆

By JEFFREY FLANAGAN

ROYALS PICK UP OPTION FOR '93, BUT DH CALLS IT A BUSINESS DECISION

October 31, 1992

While the Royals announced Friday that they have exercised their option on George Brett's contract for 1993, the message Brett said he's getting privately from the club is quite different.

And that message isn't one Brett wants to hear.

Brett said by phone from his home Friday that Royals management — he would not specify whom — is urging him to retire.

"Those people I've talked with in the Royals organization said they thought it would be better to open up a roster spot for someone younger and more deserving," Brett said. "They didn't want me back. Younger ... and more deserving? That blew me away.

"I thought for someone in my position, that was an insult. And the people I've talked to afterward about it were aghast. They thought it was an insult, too.

"It hurt. I just thought it was a strange thing to say. I didn't really know how to react. My jaw hit the floor. I didn't say anything."

Brett, 39, hasn't decided whether he will retire or return to the club for his 20th season in 1993.

Brett had a meeting with General Manager Herk Robinson on Monday but would not indicate what was discussed then.

Robinson also would not reveal the contents of Monday's discussion but said Friday: "If George wants to come back, we'd like to have him back. We exercised the option. I don't know how much clearer our signal can be."

If they hadn't exercised Brett's option by midnight Eastern time Friday, he would have become a free agent.

But Brett said the Royals' move was simply a financial maneuver. ◆

◆ Brett greets Royals owner Ewing M. Kauffman during Kauffman's induction into the Royals Hall of Fame on May 23, 1993.

KAUFFMAN APOLOGIZES TO BRETT

◆

By JEFFREY FLANAGAN

November 3, 1992

A potential feud brewing between George Brett and the Royals was defused in a flash Monday when owner Ewing Kauffman offered a public apology to Brett.

Kauffman and the Royals called a news conference Monday morning at Royals Stadium because of what Kauffman termed a misunderstanding between himself and Brett over Brett's baseball future.

Brett, who is considering retirement, was in Arizona and could not be reached for comment Monday.

The issue unfolded last week after the Royals exercised their option on Brett's contract for 1993.

Brett said Friday that the Royals were urging him to retire and were hoping to open a spot on the roster for a "younger and more deserving player."

Kauffman opened Monday's news conference with this statement:

"The reason for this meeting is that I wanted to publicly apologize to George Brett and the thousands and thousands of baseball fans throughout the country who love to see him play.

"I gave George the wrong impression in a discussion I had with him in my home and I would like to state without any equivocation whatsoever that the Royals want George Brett to play." ◆

◆ **Brett hams it up during the team photo session at his last spring training in Baseball City in 1993.**

HE'LL PLAY

◆

By JEFFREY FLANAGAN

BRETT DECIDES TO COME BACK, WILL BE WITH ROYALS IN 1993

January 7, 1993

George Brett is coming back.

Brett told *The Kansas City Star* on Wednesday he will return for his 20th season with the Royals in 1993, and he will announce those intentions at a news conference today.

Brett, who reached the 3,000-hit plateau last September, said he has not yet spoken to General Manager Herk Robinson or owner Ewing Kauffman about his decision.

Brett, 39, had been contemplating his decision to return or retire since the season ended in October.

He conferred with several present and former players, including Hall of Fame catcher Johnny Bench and former Royals pitcher Dan Quisenberry, during this off-

season but said his decision to return was influenced more by the positive reaction he received from fans.

"It was kind of strange, but every time I went through an airport or went somewhere, I had people telling me, 'Hey, come back one more year. It wouldn't be the same without you,'" Brett said by phone from his home. "Hearing those kind of things really made me feel like coming back.

"I had talked to a lot of people, and probably only about two or three said this would be a good time to cut it off. The rest just kind of said, 'Hey, if you feel you can play, then play.'"

Brett said his wife, Leslie, also encouraged him to return.

"Oh yeah, she said to go for it," Brett said. "She knew that's what I wanted to do anyway."

Brett talked to Manager Hal McRae shortly before Christmas and said McRae also gave a thumbs-up to his return.

"He told me I would hit third and DH and play every day," Brett said.

Brett has not spoken with Kauffman since the two had a discussion at Kauffman's home in November. At that meeting, Kauffman urged Brett to retire, enabling the Royals to open a spot on the roster for, Kauffman said, a "younger, more deserving player."

After that meeting was revealed in a story in *The Kansas City Star*, Kauffman and the Royals held a news conference at which Kauffman offered a public apology to Brett.

Kauffman, though, has yet to offer the apology in person or by phone to Brett.

Brett said he is eager to begin the 1993 season and began preparations for spring training by working out Wednesday at Royals Stadium.

Brett's spring-training schedule will be interrupted around March 12, which is when Leslie's baby is due. ◆

NOW RETIRING: NO. 5, BRETT

◆

By JEFFREY FLANAGAN

STAR IS MOVING TO FRONT OFFICE

September 26, 1993

George Brett had been there before, about a year ago, standing solemnly at the intersection of baseball and the rest of his life.

This time, Brett, who led the Royals to six division titles and their only World Series championship in 1985, chose the path away from playing baseball, the endeavor that forever changed his identity.

Brett, 40, announced Saturday his plans to retire from baseball at the end of this season, his 21st with the Royals, at a news conference Saturday at Kauffman Stadium.

Brett, who said he began leaning toward retirement shortly after the All-Star break in July, will play his final home game Wednesday night, and his final game next Sunday in Texas. Then he will move immediately into the club's front office as Royals vice president of baseball operations.

As vice president, a position promised under the lifetime contract he signed in 1984 with the Royals and then co-owner Avron Fogelman, Brett will have a broad range of duties, from consulting with key sponsors to evaluating Royals' players and personnel.

Brett, who is one of 19 players in baseball history with more than 3,000 hits, announced his retirement with a cracking voice and moistening eyes:

"After five days of some serious soul-searching, I have decided to retire. I always said I would not play the game for money. And I think my decision is proof of that.

"I've accomplished more in my playing days than I thought I ever would. I've played more games, gotten more hits, more home runs, played in more championship series, more All-Star Games and injured my knee more times than I ever thought I would.

"The one thing that I'm proud of most, and I say this sincerely, is spending my whole career with one team. I always and will always have respect for this organization. ...

"My baseball career is not ending. It's just taking a different direction."

Brett was flanked at the news conference by his wife, Leslie; son, Jackson; by Muriel Kauffman, the widow of late owner Ewing Kauffman; and Royals General Manager Herk Robinson.

After Brett read his statement, Kauffman turned to him and said,

◆ **George Brett announces his retirement at a press conference the afternoon before the game on September 25, 1993.**

"I love you dearly. We appreciate the way you have helped us be the best expansion team in the history of baseball.

"You even played when you were hurt, and sometimes I didn't approve of that because you were a special commodity that we wanted to keep well and healthy."

She also cited her husband's biggest thrill, when Brett hit a three-run home run off Goose Gossage that gave the Royals a three-game sweep over the Yankees in the 1980 American League playoffs.

Reaction from players and coaches was similar in tribute.

"He's just very special," Royals coach Jamie Quirk and Brett's longtime friend said through tears.

Robinson said: "The way he has gone about everything he has done in his career has meant more to the Kansas City Royals than anything possibly could."

Brett first will be eligible for election to the Hall of Fame in 1999, after he has been retired for five seasons.

Yet walking away from his playing career was not as trying as Brett had expected it to be.

"When I had a meeting with my brother Bobby and my agent (Dennis Gilbert) in Oakland on Monday," Brett said, "Bobby asked me how much it would take for me to play again. I said, 'At this time, they don't have enough money.' I had my mind made up."

Brett knew he had begun to lose his passion for the game this season.

"The game became a job," he said. "It wasn't a game anymore. And baseball shouldn't be treated that way.

"I wasn't getting that excited when I did something good, wasn't getting that down when I did something bad. I wasn't that happy when we won; I wasn't that sad when we lost. There's something missing.

"The only thing I can equate it to is if you ride the same roller coaster for 162 times, 20 years in a row, don't you want to go on another ride once in a while? I want to go on Space Mountain, Mr. Toad's Wild Ride. I'm tired.

"I think the game just beat me, which, it beats everybody in time. It beat Nolan Ryan. It took 26 years to beat Nolan. Well, it took 20 to beat me."

Brett's favorite moment?

"Probably hugging Bret Saberhagen on the mound in 1985," he said. "Winning the World Series."

Worst moment?

"Today," he said. "Right now." ◆

♦ Brett watches as his first home run goes out of Kauffman Stadium. Brett hit two home runs in this game, the day after he announced his retirement. The second homer won the game for the Royals.

BRETT SAVES PLENTY OF HIS BEST FOR LAST

◆

By DICK KAEGEL

SECOND HOMER OF DAY LIFTS ROYALS, THRILLS DEPARTING STAR

September 27, 1993

Jamie Quirk sat next to George Brett's cubicle in the Royals' clubhouse Sunday wearing a huge grin.

"There's going to be another press conference tomorrow," Quirk, a Royals coach, said wryly.

Brett arrived, grinning too, and shook his head.

"I don't have the courage to do it again," he said.

One day after emotionally announcing his retirement as a player, Brett staged one of his most memorable performances in years, slamming two home runs and a double for five RBIs.

His second homer, which carried over the right-field fence courtesy of a crosswind, came with two outs in the 10th inning and beat the California Angels 9-8.

It was a vintage, stirring, unforgettable afternoon for Brett and the fans who hung on to the end. But there will be no un-retirement.

"No second thoughts. My decision's made," Brett said firmly.

Brett was the object of at least a dozen standing ovations at Kauffman Stadium. The whooping accelerated when he doubled to right-center in the first inning, scoring Felix Jose. And again when he kayoed Angels starter John Farrell with a three-run homer to right-center field that gave the Royals a 5-3 lead in the fourth inning.

Fans left in droves after Brett grounded out in the seventh with the Royals behind 8-5, assuming he wouldn't bat again. But he did in the ninth and was hit near the left elbow by a Steve Frey pitch. That led to a three-run rally that tied the score.

The game-ending floater into the Royals' bullpen occasioned a Brett first. He left the clubhouse and returned to the field to acknowledge the remaining fans' tribute.

"I was sitting here, getting ready to uncork a cold one, and get undressed, but I figured if they stayed 10 innings on what was supposed to be a beautiful day that turned chilly and a lot of ups and downs and not a very well-played game by either side, they deserved something," Brett said.

Despite the big day, Brett had regrets.

"It's a shame you have to wait till you're eliminated to play the way you hoped to all year long," he said. "When it was needed of me to step up and be the guy, I didn't do it. Now the season's over basically, and now I can get hot. But with the announcement, it just seems like all the weight's been lifted off my shoulders — go out and enjoy yourself for the last week."

Brett certainly seemed relaxed early Sunday. He took batting practice with a homemade bat, honed in a shop class by photographer Debbie Sauer's 13-year-old son, Charlie. "Charlesville Bats" read the label.

"I've signed a new bat contract," Brett jokingly told curious teammates. "Twenty years with Louisville Slugger is enough."

And even though Brett figured that getting through the stress of his retirement announcement would guarantee sweet sleep after Saturday night's game, he was wrong. Young Jackson Richard Brett made sure of that for parents George and Leslie.

"Someone in the house was a little restless and didn't want to go to sleep," Brett said. "I said, 'Let me go get him, bring him down here and he'll sleep with us.' And it didn't work, so at 4:30 in the morning I got up and slept on the couch. I said, 'I hate to do this. I'd ride the storm with you if I didn't have a game today but I need the sleep.'"

Apparently, he got enough sleep.

His booming day Sunday extended his season-high hitting streak to 12 games (19 for 50, .380).

"When you get ovations like that, it makes you feel so good inside," Brett said. "I'm not the player I once was and I'll be the first to say that, but they still appreciate the effort and they still appreciate the success that I've had."

As Brett rounded second base in the 10th, he clenched his fist and gave the air a jubilant punch.

"I'm never going to face these guys again so you can kind of do stuff like that," Brett said. "I don't think I showed anybody up. I never intentionally show anybody up; that was just excitement." ◆

♦ Brett blows a kiss to cheering fans after he hit two homers in a game the day after he announced his retirement. Brett returned to the field as the fans chanted, "We want George."

HOW SWEET IT'S BEEN!

◆

By JO-ANN BARNAS

BIG CROWD TELLS BRETT GOODBYE

September 30, 1993

George Brett stood at the plate, the weight back on his left leg, his bat parallel to the ground, just as his mentor, Charley Lau, taught him.

He gripped the bat with his bare hands and stared at Cleveland relief pitcher Jeremy Hernandez.

The stance. The look. The moment.

The last time, too.

And, it happened. Brett sent a ground-ball single into center field driving in the tying run.

Brett made his 1,366th and final appearance Wednesday night at Kauffman Stadium, and he left us with a magical moment.

What followed the Royals' 3-2 victory was a homespun tribute that could have lasted well into the night if the 36,999 fans had anything to do with it.

Fireworks exploded in the sky when it was over. Brett jumped into a golf cart for one last trip around the field. Fans leaned over the railing, and Brett extended his right arm, saluting them.

When the cart stopped, Brett got off and kissed home plate.

As the crowd cried "George! George! George!" Brett's teammates hoisted him onto the shoulders of Mike Macfarlane and Mark Gubicza for one last heartfelt tribute.

No, Brett won't forget Wednesday. Not the cheers. Not the hundreds of flashbulbs that lit up the stadium every time he was in view.

"I'm sure it was a moment I'll never forget," Brett said. "Driving around in the golf cart, the fans' reaction obviously made me feel very warm and very appreciated over the years.

"It was a good feeling, no doubt about it. It's something I'll never forget."

For the fans who were there, it was their one last look, one last time to say goodbye to No. 5.

How to summarize two decades in a moment? How do you capture the full essence of the greatest baseball player ever to pull on a Royals uniform?

The fans did it the only way they knew how. They gave him a

◆ **Brett gets his final hit in Kauffman Stadium against the Cleveland Indians.**

Joe Ledford

standing ovation. Not once, but every time he stepped onto the field.

"He's the whole Kansas City team to us," said teary-eyed Bonnie Maple, 81, a baseball season-ticket holder for 33 years.

"It's happy and sad both. George has just been a part of all of us for so long."

It seemed just as hard to Brett to say goodbye. He said as much last Saturday when he announced his retirement, although he kept stressing he won't really be gone. He'll still be active in his new job as vice president/baseball operations. In fact, he will travel with Herk Robinson to the general manager's meeting in November in Florida.

"I can still play, but not like I once did," Brett said during his pre-game news conference. "The game has become a job to me. The game deserves better."

Brett realized during the summer that greatness alone can't turn back the clock; that when spirit and will can't stretch a single into a double, it's time to move on.

Still, many of his closest friends weren't convinced.

"I would test him as the season went along," said Jamie Quirk, a Royals coach and one of Brett's closest friends. "In Oakland (last Monday) he hit an opposite-field home run. He came back to the dugout and I said, 'You're going to play again, right?

"He answered, 'No.'

"Even now, it seems strange. Not to see George Brett in a Royals uniform will take some getting used to."

But while Brett was confident of his decision, ending a career in which he has collected 3,153 hits — a sure pass into the Hall of Fame — it didn't make his last drive to Kauffman Stadium any easier. For him. Or his fans.

Brett's day began normal enough. Coffee and the crossword puzzle. A bridge game and d'Bronx deli for lunch.

He left his house at 3:10 p.m., with his older brother John, who along with two other brothers and their mother, Ethel Johnson, came to Kansas City for the final game.

As Brett drove past Mission Hills Country Club on his way to the ballpark, he turned to John and said, "Maybe next year at this time, I'll be there playing golf."

"It's a weird feeling today, knowing that it's going to be all over," said John Brett, 47. ◆

◆ Teammates hug Brett after his final game at Kauffman Stadium.

LAST TOUCH OF HOME CAPS BRETT FAREWELL

◆

By DICK KAEGEL

KISSING THE PLATE IS FITTING FAREWELL GESTURE AFTER WINNING KC FINALE

October 1, 1993

When it was over, after he'd gotten the game-tying hit, toured the stadium in a golf cart and acknowledged the fans Wednesday night, George Brett got to his knees in the batter's box.

Bending down, he kissed home plate.

Then Brett grinned, waved one last time to the crowd, slapped hands with his teammates and was hoisted to the shoulders of pitcher Mark Gubicza and catcher Mike Macfarlane.

Could there have been a more fitting farewell for the greatest player in Royals history?

"It was very special. I'm sure it's a moment I'll never forget," Brett said. "Driving around in the golf cart, the fans' reaction obviously made me feel very warm and very

appreciated over the years. It was a good feeling, no doubt about it."

The idea of kissing home plate came to Brett by way of Hank Bauer, a crusty former manager and scout, and Jamie Quirk, now a Royals coach.

"Hank Bauer used to tell Jamie Quirk that he should kiss home plate every time he comes to the ballpark so I figured that the last time in uniform I thought I'd kiss home plate and tell Jamie what he was missing," Brett said.

What was he missing?

"Nothing special, nothing special," Brett replied, grinning.

After Brett delivered a bouncing single that tied the Cleveland Indians 2-2 in the eighth inning, he moved to second base on a walk to Bob Hamelin. That's when Manager Hal McRae sent out rookie Phil Hiatt as a pinch runner for Brett.

"Booooooo," said the fans before quickly shifting into a standing ovation for Brett.

Brett said he understood the move; it's one that McRae frequently has used in the late innings with the game on the line.

Still, the fans grumbled, because who could say that Brett wouldn't bat again, perhaps in the ninth with a chance to win it?

"I can understand the fans," McRae said. "They came to see him play, to see him hit. That probably put another 18,000 fans in the stands. It was an emotional night. But my main concern was to win the ballgame."

But, as McRae noted, Brett came out after an RBI single — something to remember for his final at-bat in Kansas City.

And the point became moot when Kevin Koslofski's game-ending hit left Brett's No. 3 spot, now occupied by Hiatt, two batters away.

Brett, after going hitless in his first three at-bats, was determined as he faced Jeremy Hernandez in the eighth with Koslofski on second base.

"The adrenaline was flowing a little too much like it has the last couple days and I was trying to do too much," he said. "The one thing I didn't want to do was go out and leave another runner in scoring position like I did in the first inning when I flew out to left field.

"So I contributed to the team's victory, tied it up for us, and Kevin Koslofski got the big hit to win it in the ninth. But just to be a part of it and for the 39 or 40,000 to go home happy and for me to go home happy was a big thrill."

McRae was asked what the chances were that he'd manage a player of Brett's caliber again.

"Nil," he said. "They don't put good wood in them anymore." ◆

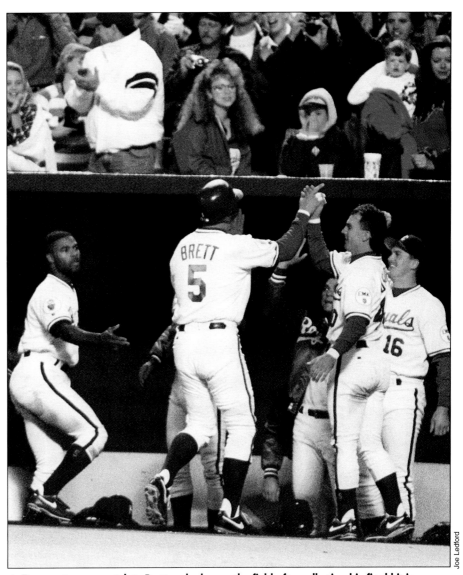

◆ **Teammates congratulate Brett as he leaves the field after collecting his final hit in Kauffman Stadium.**

◆ **Fans showed their feelings for Brett at his last home game.**

◆ Brett tips his helmet to Rangers fans after his final major-league hit on October 3.

CAREER COMES TO PERFECT CONCLUSION

◆

By DICK KAEGEL

BRETT'S LAST AT-BAT IS HIT; ROYALS WIN

October 4, 1993

ARLINGTON, Texas — For George Brett, could it have ended a more appropriate way? Single up the middle, base hit No. 3,154, in the last at-bat of a superlative career.

Then Brett, on Gary Gaetti's home run, trotted around the bases for the last time Sunday as he put the finishing touches on his 20-plus seasons with the Royals in a 4-1 victory over the Texas Rangers.

"It found a hole up the middle," Brett said. "Good way to end a career."

It was a bouncer, just to the left-field side of second base, with shortstop Manuel Lee watching the ball skip past. Not a rocket, not a homer, not a double — but a hit.

"It didn't matter," he said. "I wanted to stand on first one time."

This, he declared, was his most emotional at-bat ever. He had gone hitless in 11 previous at-bats in this series. He hadn't connected since going out in Kansas City in the same manner, single up the middle.

"The adrenaline was going and I was nervous," Brett said. "I knew it was my last at-bat, the ovation and things like that. My eyes watered up, my throat didn't get dry, though. I wished it would have and my eyes would have been clear."

As Brett left the dugout to lead off the ninth, Royals coach Jamie Quirk exchanged glances with his longtime pal. Rangers reliever Tom Henke was warming up on the mound. After Brett reached the on-deck circle, Quirk called over batboy Ryan Bresette.

"I told Ryan to remind George who I got my last at-bat against," Quirk said. "It was Tom Henke."

The batboy delivered the message.

"He turned around and looked at Jamie in the dugout, and they both smiled," Bresette said.

Meanwhile, all the fans in Arlington Stadium on the ballpark's last day and players in both dugouts were giving Brett a standing ovation. The Rangers, like the Royals, came to the top step to applaud.

"I thought that was a class gesture, especially with the feuds we've had with them this year," pitcher David Cone said.

◆ During his final major-league game at Arlington Stadium Rangers fans said goodbye.

Jim McTaggart

In the midst of all this, Nolan Ryan, who had just been honored by a highlight tape on the stadium screen, popped out of the Rangers' dugout to wave his cap. The two future Hall of Famers, who had exchanged lineup cards at home plate before the game, were going out together even though Ryan was unable to pitch.

Henke, employing fastballs, threw one high and inside for ball one. Brett swung and missed the next pitch, then hit a foul into the stands near third base.

"I was going hard after George," Henke said. "He's a true competitor and he wouldn't want it any other way. I'm not going to walk him, that wouldn't be fair. I just threw strikes and went after him."

Gaetti, watching from the dugout, didn't know how Brett was doing it.

"I wondered how he was hitting because I was getting teary-eyed, too," Gaetti said.

On the 1-2 pitch, Brett skipped the ball past the mound and into center field. He arrived at first base, grinned and acknowledged the cheers.

"I was just happy to be standing there," Brett said. "I swung at a ball over my head, fouled off a good pitch to hit, then swung at a ball up and away and dribbled it though the middle."

Previously, against Rangers starter Steve Dreyer, Brett had flied out twice to left field and grounded out to second base. The grounder to second was how Brett often described how he wanted his last at-bat to go, so he could hustle down the line one more time to show the youngsters how it should be done.

But that, it developed, would not be his last chance.

After Brett's single, Bob Hamelin looked at strike three. Gaetti then pounded an 0-2 Henke pitch into the left-center-field seats, his 14th homer since joining the Royals in late June.

"I didn't want the old guy to have to run too hard," Gaetti said. "He might as well cruise on in."

But, on this cloudy, unusually cool Sunday afternoon in Texas, Brett was still a player. He wanted one more hit and got it.

"It wasn't pretty," Brett said. "I wish it was a line drive somewhere but, you know, beggars can't be choosy. I was struggling a little bit, so I was just happy to touch first base today." ◆

LAST HIT PAID TRIBUTE TO AN UNMATCHED CAREER

◆

By GIB TWYMAN

October 4, 1993

ARLINGTON, Texas — For 21 years, the Lord has given us this day our daily Brett.

Now he has been taken away.

And that, my good friends and neighbors, is it.

Give No. 5 one last high five. You will never see another like him in our town.

Did you get the finality of that word, never? Good.

Every now and then I hear "probably won't" and "maybe not" creep into conversations about Brett. Forget those words. There'll never be another George Brett, period.

This goes far beyond numbers, imposing as they are. Brett will go down as the only man in history with 3,000 hits, 600 doubles, 100 triples, 300 homers and 200 stolen bases. And the only one to win batting titles in three decades (1976, 1980, 1990).

Some day, some kid may come along who strings together some serious years for us. He'll never be another Brett.

The economics work against a guy staying with one team more than a few years, much less 20. And with Ewing Kauffman's industrial-strength deep pockets gone, KC might have trouble holding a franchise player.

But mostly we'll never see another Brett because, uniquely, he had the "whole package" as a superstar. He was great in the game, great with teammates and great with fans and reporters.

With his statistics, Brett easily could have taken on an I-am-the-star attitude. Instead, he was the first guy to take rookies under his wing.

I know, I know, someone out there undoubtedly got stiffed on an autograph request. But no athlete can honor every request. Brett was diligent about autographs. If he made someone feel bad, then it was leaving the 201st after signing 200. You can't avoid that.

Brett had a couple celebrated run-ins with news media representatives. But on balance, he bent over backward for the press, and he was so quotable he almost couldn't help himself.

"I know I had my bad moments here and there," Brett said. "But when I took that last trip around the (Kauffman) stadium in the golf cart, it was like all was forgotten."

The thing we won't forget is Brett in the big moments. He danced with destiny again Sunday in his last at-bat against Texas.

He'd gone zero for 11 since getting a hit Wednesday in his last at-bat at Kauffman Stadium. Now, either Brett was going to finish out ohfer-Texas, or he was going to do something to make us remember.

◆ **Brett leaves Arlington Stadium after his final major-league game.**

He got a hit.

But the way it happened offers a fascinating insight into the way baseball works and the impression Brett has made on his game the last 21 years.

Tom Henke was out there, a smoke-throwing country boy from rural Missouri, one of the premier relievers in baseball. And to make matters more interesting, Brett was fighting the biggest case of nerves he'd ever had.

"It was my most emotional at-bat of my life," he said.

At 4:09, he walked to the batter's box. Overcast, 72 degrees, wind slightly toward right. As he dug in, his teammates came as one to the top of the dugout.

"Nothing planned. Totally spontaneous," Jamie Quirk said.

Nolan Ryan came out and doffed his cap emphatically at Brett. The Rangers all were at the top step now. Brett didn't see them. Just his guys.

"My eyes were filling up," he said. "I said to myself, 'These guys are really into this last at-bat.' I wanted to do something special. I didn't want to strike out."

Henke had made up his mind to throw Brett nothing but fastballs. No nasty forkballs. He brought high heat the first pitch. High and outside. Ball one. Second pitch, more heat. Brett swung through. Strike one.

It wasn't until then that Henke got his message through: Nothing but fastballs, George.

"He nodded at me. I winked back at him," Henke said.

The next fastball, Brett slung foul. And the next one, he bounced up the middle.

The eyes told you that Manny Lee, the Texas shortstop, could have caught the ball. He broke late to his left and didn't extend well as the ball went past.

Years from now, people may remember that hit as a solid single to center. Even if it's recalled as a catchable bouncer through the box, it won't matter much. Not much at all.

You know what that hit was? It was pure tribute to Brett from the very guys who'd give it most grudgingly — his opponents.

It was their nod, their we-are-not-worthy bow, if you will.

They, like us, knew they'd never see another one like him. ◆

FIVE MAGICAL MOMENTS FOR NO. 5

1

October 10, 1980:

Kansas City 4, New York 2

Late Royals owner Ewing Kauffman called this game the most memorable in team history. The Royals swept away three years of playoff frustration against the New York Yankees when Brett hit a three-run home run off Goose Gossage, wiping out a 2-1 Yankees lead in the top of the seventh inning. The 4-2 victory gave the Royals a sweep of the American League Championship Series and their first pennant.

"I didn't feel that much pressure," Brett said, "because you knew what you were going to get. He threw a 98-mile-per-hour fastball and a slider that was about 95. I just had to get my bat tuned up to 95 or 98."

2

October 11, 1985:

Kansas City 6, Toronto 5

Playoff frustration again was setting in for the Royals in game three of the championship series against Toronto at Royals Stadium. They had lost the first two games of the best-of-seven series to the Blue Jays and had not won a playoff game since the pennant clincher in 1980. Brett changed all of that and started the Royals on the way to their first World Series title with one of the best performances in postseason history.

He dominated the game with both his bat and his glove. At the plate he singled, doubled, hit two home runs, scored four runs and drove in three. In the field he made a sensational backhanded stop in foul territory behind third base and threw out Damaso Garcia at the plate, snuffing out a third-inning rally. Brett's second home run tied the score 5-5 in the sixth inning and inspired his teammates.

"We're in the driver's seat now," Jamie Quirk said. "George has one more at-bat." He was right. Brett's final at-bat produced a single that started the game-winning rally.

♦ Brett acknowledges the crowd at ceremonies before his final home game at Kauffman Stadium.

Jim McTaggart

3

July 24, 1983:

Kansas City 5, New York 4

Brett's career was marked by postseason heroics, but his most famous home run probably was the one he hit in a somewhat meaningless game in mid-1983. In a moment similar to his homer in the 1980 playoffs, Brett hit a two-run shot off Goose Gossage that apparently gave the Royals a 5-4 lead over New York with two outs in the top of the ninth inning at Yankee Stadium. Yankees Manager Billy Martin, however, complained that Brett's bat had pine tar on the handle exceeding the 18-inch maximum, and the umpires agreed and called Brett out. Brett's charge from the dugout to argue the call, shown countless times since on baseball highlight tapes, touched off a wild scene at home plate.

"I don't remember any of it," Brett said. "All I know about is what I've seen on tapes.

It's probably the one time in my life where I got so mad, everything just blanked out."

American League President Lee MacPhail later reversed the umpire's decision, ruling the play a home run because Brett had not violated "… the spirit of the rules." The game resumed Aug. 18 without Brett, who was ejected for his rampage, and the Royals finished off a 5-4 victory.

4

September 30, 1992:

Kansas City 4, California 0

Brett achieved a personal milestone in his trademark dramatic style. After missing two games because of a shoulder injury, Brett became the 18th player to achieve 3,000 hits by rapping out four hits in Anaheim, Calif. The milestone hit came in the seventh inning on a one-hop single past Angels second baseman Ken Oberkfell.

"It happened so quick, I really didn't have time to prepare for it," Brett said. "But I'm relieved, very relieved."

5

August 17, 1980:

Kansas City 8, Toronto 3

Brett grabbed the attention of the nation on a Sunday afternoon at Royals Stadium by moving his batting average over .400, a moment that began a race to become the first player since Ted Williams in 1941 to finish a season above .400.

Brett smacked a double in the eighth inning that boosted his average to .401 and then stood at second base and accepted an ovation from the crowd. The chase for .400 took a toll on Brett as the media attention mounted late in the season.

"There were times I felt like half the United States was in my house," he said. He finished the year at .390, the highest in the major leagues since Williams. ♦

◆ Brett spent his final season with former teammate Hal McRae as the Royals' manager.

A CONVERSATION WITH
GEORGE BRETT

◆

October 4, 1993

Since 1973 George Brett has been creating memories for baseball fans in general and Royals fans in particular. But what about *his* memories? In a conversation last week with Dick Kaegel and Jeff Flanagan, baseball reporters for *The Kansas City Star*, Brett looks back on his playing career. It ended Sunday in Arlington, Texas, the end of a hectic week beginning September 25 when Brett announced his retirement at a news conference at Royals Stadium.

LEAVING THE DUGOUT

Star: Is this the way you envisioned your retirement would unfold?

Brett: More hectic. Much more hectic. Phone is ringing off the hook. I did something for Channel 4 the other night and now, of course, Channel 5 and 9 want to do something, too. Friends coming into Texas, need more rooms.

It's just been a hectic couple more days. It comes in good to have a wife that cares about you and it helps out good that you have a little boy in the house to help you take your mind off things.

Star: Have you been able to sleep?

Brett: I've been able to sleep since I made the announcement. Before then, I had a tough time sleeping. Every day in Oakland, it was tough.

Star: Any second thoughts at all?

Brett: None. None at all.

Star: Even after you hit two home runs last Sunday?

Brett: No. I made the right decision, and I stand by it.

Star: It's been said that you would never leave the game as long as you were still hitting the ball hard. And lately, you've been hitting it hard.

Brett: I have been hitting it hard. But I think that has made it easier. I always said I wanted to go out on my terms, not their terms.

I've struggled to hit the last three years, since 1990. Failed to hit .300. I really didn't have a hot streak this year, really didn't have one last year. And just the lack of consistency drove me away. I just thought it was time. I know I'm going out when I can still

◆ **Brett ... never tries to rank the great moments.**

Joe Ledford

play. But I won't put myself in position where I can hit .220. That's not how I wanted to go out.

Star: The Royals offered a pretty good chunk of money to have you back, nearly $3 million. How can anyone walk away from that?

Brett: I can. I did. I won't play this game just for money.

THE NEW JOB

Star: How do you envision the vice president position with the Royals?

Brett: To have some say in who's on the team and who gets traded and who doesn't get traded, but not a job where you spend eight hours a day or nine hours a day in the office when the team is on the road or 12 hours a day when the team's at home.

Star: This obviously will be a much more meaningful position than Ewing Kauffman had projected.

Brett: I think Mr. Kauffman didn't realize he was wrong in the meeting last October we had with him, about going out and selling tickets for the Lancers. He didn't realize he wouldn't be getting the full utilization out of me. And he did say that (he was wrong) when I talked with him this summer.

And I hope to have some say in the decision-making process. Herk (Robinson) already has invited me to the general managers' meeting in Naples (Fla.) at the end of October, which I will probably go to. That's even though I'm not a general manager, I do report to the general manager with my findings or my ideas.

Star: Is the fact that this is another challenge appeal to you the most?

Brett: Well, you have to do something. You have to do something with your life. So many people have told me that 'Hey, retirement sounds great, but you have to do something besides play golf every day.' And I have found something else to do.

I think it will be a great marriage. Like I've said, my career isn't ending, it's just taking a new direction.

Star: Would you ever want to be an owner or part owner of the Royals?

Brett (laughing): No. They lose too much money. Don't you read the paper?

REACHING MILESTONES

Star: You've had so much packed into the 21 years — the World Series, the playoffs, the run at .400, the pine tar, the batting titles, the homers off Goose Gossage — is it all just a blur or can you sort it all out?

Brett: I can pretty much replay those things in my mind and remember the feelings and the emotions and get goose bumps to this day for the things you just said and get tears in my eyes for the way I felt and the way my teammates felt, like the World Series, or the first time we beat the Yankees in 1980.

But this year, I have one memory. Just one memory. The game last Sunday. One memory. That's the only memory I have. I won't remember anything else. That's something I'll always remember. Look — I've got goose bumps right now.

Star: But the best one of all time was hugging Bret Saberhagen after the 1985 World Series?

Brett: For the first time in my life, 25 guys got together and got to celebrate something very, very special. Winning the pennant in 1980 was very special, but it wasn't the ultimate.

Winning the World Series is the ultimate for a baseball player, and I feel sorry for the guys like Cookie (Rojas) and Ernie Banks and the guys that played years and years in the major leagues and never got a chance to play in one, let alone win one. I had a chance in my 20-year career to play in two, and it should have been three or four with the teams we had.

But all the memories that you said go back three years minimum. Winning the third batting title in 1990 was the last big memory. Nothing happened in '91, nothing happened in '92.

Star: Not even the 3,000th hit last year?

Brett: Yeah, that's right. I forgot about that.

Star: Have you ever tried to rank those memories?

Brett: No, I don't even try. I can't. They are just very special memories that I'll have for years.

DEALING WITH REPORTERS

Star: Have you ever fantasized what it would be like to play in a big market like Chicago or LA or New York?

Brett: No, because it never happened, and it will never happen.

Star: Are you grateful you were able to avoid the daily media circus in those towns?

Brett: Definitely. That's one of the things that attracted me to Kansas City. I got a taste of what it was in New York being around in the playoffs. Kansas City is just a laid-back, Midwestern town

♦ During George Brett's last game in Kauffman Stadium, Royals players wore their pants high on their legs with the number five on their socks.

Steve Gonzales

that if you don't want a lot of publicity, and you don't want everyone to know about your life, you couldn't find a better place to play, maybe with the exception of Milwaukee.

The media here are so fair, back there there's so much controversy. I think the media back there strive for that controversy. But here, they just report the truth.

Star: You've had very few run-ins with media types in your career.

Brett: I hit a photographer once with a crutch in the head one time, and I had a fight with a (newspaper) reporter in a lobby of a hotel once. But that all comes with maturing and dealing with becoming a celebrity or recognizable person.

You find out the more successful you are, the more newsworthy you become. It was hard to deal with at first. But I've accepted it now.

But as far as dealing with the media on a one-to-one basis, I've never had any problem.

Star: When did you stop reading what was written about yourself?

Brett: When you first make it up to the major leagues and you win a game, you want to go out and read a paper and see what they say about you. That's positive reinforcement, and it works for you.

After a while, it wasn't that big a deal any more. You had already done it, you knew what the paper was going to say. I didn't start subscribing to the paper until about five years ago. I used to always pack up and go home after the season, and during the season, I didn't want 10 newspapers sitting in my driveway during road trips.

I did read it Sunday (day after retirement). It made me feel good, to see what my teammates said. You can hear what your teammates say, but when you read it, it's a little different. It's a tremendous compliment. It makes you feel warm inside.

BUSINESS OF SPORTS

Star: You've never seemed enticed by the big endorsements, like other superstars.

Brett: I did Puma, signed a big contract with them years ago. Things didn't go well for them financially. Ended up, when my contract was over, just wearing Nikes. I don't even have a shoe contract. Lot of guys have shoe contracts, but I don't even have one.

That's not by my design. I would love to have one, because if you have a shoe contract, they pay you to wear their shoes. I don't get anything from Nike.

As far as the big endorsement goes, I did a lot when I was young. The 1980 thing was the crowning blow of my celebrity status with the run at .400. Did the 7-Up, the Gillette, the Lifebuoy soap and some national ads, and this year I did some Ben-Gay.

It wasn't always important to me. People always said, 'You should be doing more.' I'm not a guy who tries to go out and solicit myself. If somebody wants me to work for them, they come to me. I don't have an agent out there scratching doors.

Star: Why not, with all the money available?

Brett: I always said that the money isn't the most important thing. I probably surprised a lot of people by turning down the contract for next year.

DEALING WITH MR. K

Star: What about your relationship with Mr. Kauffman? Was it good when you first came to Kansas City?

Brett: It was good, very good. I think the friction started back in 1981, when we went on strike. That's when it started. I think that's when he started losing interest in the ballplayers. And then I think the close relationship I had with Mr. Fogelman may have rubbed him the wrong way a little. The meeting I had with (Mr. K) in his office this summer, roughly two months before he passed away, was very positive.

And the meeting we had last October was very positive for the first 10 minutes. He was speaking to me like a father to a son. And, I'll remember him like that.

Star: Some people have speculated that your relationship was a little bit like father and son?

Brett: I didn't see it that way.

BRETT'S HITTING MENTOR

Star: So much has been written and discussed about your relationship with Charley Lau.

Brett: Well, Steve Boros and I were talking about that just the other day. He was asking me who the biggest influence was in my career, do you think it was Charley? And I said 'Yeah, no doubt in my mind.'

Steve saw me play in Instructional League in 1971 and 1972, and I was a completely different-type hitter then. I was a decent hitter in the minor leagues, but I never hit .300. And Charley basically built me a foundation that allowed me to stay in the major leagues for 20 years, using his theories.

Plus, he was like a father figure to me. I grew up in southern California, and I got here and really knew nobody in town when I first moved here. Charley always had an arm out for me. There was taking extra batting practice with him, playing cards with him, going out on the road and having a beer with him after games. We just developed a very special friendship.

♦ Brett's uniform hangs at his locker before his last home game.

It was so special that he had two Royals that were pallbearers at his funeral, and it was me and Hal McRae. That's how strong he felt about us.

About three days before he passed away, we were in spring training at Fort Myers, and we got a call from his wife in the Keys and she said, 'If you want to see Charley while he's still living, you better jump in an airplane and come right away.'

So we flew down right away. Chartered a little three-seater, saw him and he died about three days later. It was real hard.

Star: You never would have had the career without Charley?

Brett: No. No doubt in my mind. I don't think I would have played 20 years or won the batting titles. The time he started working with me I was hitting .200 in 200 at-bats at the All-Star break in 1974. I wound up hitting .282. The goal was to hit .250, and I hit .282, and they fired him with three days to go. I wound up going 0 for my last 12. I guess he was my security blanket at first. I was upset.

ALL IN THE FAMILY

Star: A lot of misinformation has been spread over the years about your relationship with your brothers and your father. How are your relationships with your brothers now?

Brett: My brothers and I are very close. There was a lot of competition between us growing up, trying to be as good as Ken. Ken was clearly the best athlete in the family.

My brother John had the most desire. Bobby was very gifted. And I was the worst athlete of all of us, from what I've been told. But evidently I had the biggest drive. I'd listen and work and try to get accolades from my father and from my brothers. I've never really gotten them to this day.

Star: Would (your father) be proud of you right now?

Brett: He'd probably want me to keep playing. I know he'd be here right now.

Star: Is there a part of you that wishes he was here right now?

Brett: I know it's not possible. He was a very big influence on my life. Just like my mother was. And my mother is here. My mother was the peacekeeper of the house, which you need with four brothers. When you felt like you weren't wanted, my mother would tell you that she loved you.

Star: What's your proudest moment, professional or personal?

Brett: A tie. My marriage and the birth of my son. Getting married was the biggest change in my life, and having a son and that responsibility for the rest of my life was the biggest joy. ♦

BRETT'S PITCHERS HIT LIST

Don Aase-8
Glenn Abbott-14
Jim Abbott-17
Paul Abbott-1
Jim Acker-3
Juan Agosto-2
Rick Aguilera-4
Vic Albury-7
Scott Aldred-1
Doyle Alexander-25
Gerald Aledander-2
Brian Allard-1
Allan Anderson-4
Luis Aponte-2
Jack Armstrong-1
Brad Arnsberg-1
Fernando Arroyo-4
Keith Atherton-4
Don August-5
Jerry Augustine-5
Rick Austin-1
Bob Babcock-3
Stan Bahnsen-6
Scott Bailes-4
Howard Bailey-1
Doug Bair-2
Steve Baker-1
Jeff Ballard-3
Eddie Bane-4
Scott Bankhead-3
Willie Banks-3
Floyd Bannister-24
Ray Bare-4
John Barfield-1
Len Barker-11
Jeff Barkley-2
Mike Barlow-3
Salome Barojas-2
Jim Barr-2
Steve Barr-1
Francisco Barrios-12
Ross Baumgarten-1
Jose Bautista-5
Dave Beard-4
Jim Beattie-6
Andy Beene-1
Fred Beene-1
Eric Bell-2
Jason Bere-5
Juan Berenguer-6
Sean Bergman-2
Karl Best-1
Jim Bibby-3
Mike Bielecki-1
Jack Billingham-5
Doug Bird-2
Mike Birkbeck-3
Tim Birtsas-1
Joe Bitker-2
Jeff Bittiger-1
Bud Black-1
Vida Blue-22
Bert Blyleven-27
Mike Boddicker-12
Tommy Boggs-2
Brian Bohanon-1
Tom Bolton-5
Mark Bomback-2
Ricky Bones-4
Rich Bordi-1
Chris Bosio-16
Dick Bosman-2
Dennis Boyd-15
Tom Brennan-3
Ken Brett-6
Nelson Briles-4

Pete Broberg-8
Jackie Brown-6
Kevin Brown-15
Mike Brown-2
DeWayne Buice-2
Tom Burgmeier-10
Steve Burke-2
Tim Burke-1
Britt Burns-14
Todd Burns-2
Ray Burris-2
Tom Buskey-3
John Butcher-11
Bill Butler-5
Marty Bystrom-1
Greg Cadaret-6
Mike Caldwell-14
Bill Campbell-6
Mike Campbell-2
John Candelaria-2
Tom Candiotti-7
George Cappuzzello-1
Steve Carlton-1
Chuck Cary-5
Larry Casian-2
Tony Castillo-1
Bill Castro-5
Bill Caudill-2
Jose Cecena-1
John Cerutti-4
Ray Chadwick-1
Billy Champion-3
Jim Clancy-34
Bryan Clark-3
Mark Clark-1
Ken Clay-6
Mark Clear-2
Roger Clemens-19
Pat Clements-4
Reggie Cleveland-7
David Clyde-2
Chris Codiroli-5
Jim Colborn-9
Joe Coleman-7
Steve Comer-9
Keith Comstock-1
Arnaldo Contreras-2
Jim Converse-2
Dennis Cook-2
Doug Corbett-2
Ed Correa-1
Joe Cowley-1
Jim Crawford-2
Steve Crawford-1
Keith Creel-2
Chuck Crim-1
Victor Cruz-1
Mike Cuellar-4
John Cumberland-1
Ron Darling-6
Danny Darwin-13
Bob Darwin-1
Joel Davis-2
Ron Davis-8
Storm Davis-9
Bill Dawley-1
Joe Decker-9
Jose DeLeon-1
Rich DeLucia-4
John Denny-4
Jim Deshaies-1
Ken Dixon-5
Chuck Dobson-3
Pat Dobson-6
John Doherty-1
John Dopson-3
Richard Dotson-14
Kelly Downs-5
Doug Drabek-1
Dick Drago-9

Rob Dressler-3
Tim Drummond-1
Brian DuBois-1
Mike Dunne-1
Mike Dyer-1
Jamie Easterly-3
Dennis Eckersley-19
Tom Edens-1
Juan Eichelberger-2
Mark Eichhorn-2
Dave Eiland-3
Dock Ellis-1
Steve Ellsworth-4
Roger Erickson-10

Scott Erickson-7
Ed Farmer-2
John Farrell-4
Alex Fernandez-9
Bob Ferris-2
Mark Fidrych-1
Ed Figueroa-25
Tom Filer-3
Pete Filson-3
Rollie Fingers-6
Chuck Finley-11
Brian Fisher-3
Mike Flanagan-29
Dave Fleming-2
Ray Fontenot-2
Dave Ford-1
Ken Forsch-1
Terry Forster-5
Tim Fortugno-2
Tony Fossas-3
Steve Foucault-4
Willie Fraser-6
George Frazier-1
Dave Freisleben-1
Todd Frohwirth-2
Dave Frost-9
Bob Galasso-1
Ramon Garcia-1
Mike Gardiner-3
Wes Gardner-3
Wayne Garland-3
Jerry Garvin-6
Dave Geisel-3
Bob L. Gibson-1

Paul Gibson-2
Jerry Don Gleaton-2
Dave Goltz-26
German Gonzalez-1
Rich Gossage-10
Jim Gott-7
Mauro Gozzo-1
Joe Grahe-1
Mike Griffin-2
Steve Grilli-4
Jason Grimsley-1
Ross Grimsley-11
Cecilio Guante-1
Eddie Guardado-3

Lee Guetterman-7
Ron Guidry-18
Don Gullett-4
Bill Gullickson-4
Larry Gura-2
Mark Guthrie-7
Jose Guzman-11
Juan Guzman-4
Moose Haas-12
David Haas-1
Dave Hamilton-5
Bill Hands-2
Erik Hanson-8
Steve Hargan-4
Pete Harnisch-4
Gene Harris-3
Greg Allen Harris-2
Roric Harrison-2
Chuck Hartenstein-1
Mike Hartley-1
Paul Hartzell-13
Andy Hassler-5
Tom Hausman-1
Brad Havens-2
Andy Hawkins-6
Ray Hayward-3
Neal Heaton-6
Dave Heaverlo-3
Gorman Heimueller-3
Tom Henke-5
Mike Henneman-2
Doug Henry-1
Willie Hernandez-4
Jeremy Hernandez-2

Roberto Hernandez-1
Greg Hibbard-7
Ted Higuera-9
Shawn Hillegas-5
John Hiller-10
Rich Hinton-1
Sterling Hitchcock-1
Ed Hodge-2
Joe Hoerner-1
Guy Hoffman-1
Jeff Holly-2
Brian Holman-7
Darren Holmes-3
Brian Holton-1

Ken Holtzman-7
Rick Honeycutt-16
Don Hood-5
Burt Hooton-3
Vince Horsman-1
Charlie Hough-23
Tom House-5
Fred Howard-1
Steve Howe-1
Jay Howell-3
LaMarr Hoyt-5
Charlie Hudson-1
Phil Huffman-5
Jim Hughes-11
James Hunter-2
Catfish Hunter-13
Bruce Hurst-10
Darrell Jackson-1
Grant Jackson-3
Roy Lee Jackson-3
Bob James-2
Domingo Jean-1
Mike Jeffcoat-6
Jesse Jefferson-15
Ferguson Jenkins-19
Miguel Jimenez-1
Tommy John-11
Bart Johnson-4
David C. Johnson-2
David W. Johnson-4
Jeff Johnson-2
John Henry Johnson-4
Randy Johnson-1
Tom Johnson-7

Barry Jones-1
Calvin Jones-1
Jimmy Jones-2
Odell Jones-2
Rick Jones-3
Jim Kaat-11
Scott Kamieniecki-4
Curt Kaufman-1
Rickey Keeton-1
Mike Kekich-2
Matt Keough-12
Jim Kern-1
Joe Kerrigan-1
Jimmy Key-9
Dana Kiecker-3
Paul Kilgus-4
Eric King-4
Brian Kingman-8
Mike Kinnunen-1
Don Kirkwood-8
Bruce Kison-7
Joe Klink-2
Chris Knapp-14
Kurt Knudsen-1
Mark Knudson-3
Kevin Kobel-4
Jerry Koosman-9
Randy Kramer-1
Tom Kramer-2
Ken Kravec-9
Bill Krueger-7
Jack Kucek-1
Jerry Kutzler-1
Bob Lacey-1
Pete Ladd-2
Lerrin LaGrow-7
Dennis Lamp-7
Dick Lange-5
Rick Langford-15
Mark Langston-9
Dave LaPoint-6
Dave LaRoche-6
Gary Lavelle-3
Bill Laxton-1
Jack Lazorko-1
Charlie Lea-1
Terry Leach-1
Luis Leal-10
Tim Leary-4
Bill Lee-5
Mark Lee-1
Craig Lefferts-2
Phil Leftwich-2
Charlie Leibrandt-1
Dave Leiper-2
Al Leiter-1
Mark Leiter-5
Dave Lemanczyk-4
Mark Lemongello-3
Randy Lerch-4
Dennis Lewallyn-1
Scott Lewis-1
Derek Lilliquist-5
Paul Lindblad-6
Graeme Lloyd-1
Skip Lockwood-3
Mickey Lolich-2
Tim Lollar-2
Bill Long-3
Aurelio Lopez-3
Mike Loynd-2
Gary Lucas-1
Urbano Lugo-2
Sparky Lyle-6
Rick Lysander-2
Frank MacCormack-2
Bob MacDonald-3
Julio Machado-1
Mickey Mahler-1
Pat Mahomes-2

Tom Makowski-1
Mike Marshall-2
Dennis Martinez-23
Fred Martinez-2
Tippy Martinez-3
Mike Mason-7
Terry Mathews-1
Jon Matlack-15
Rudy May-4
Tom McCarthy-1
Kirk McCaskill-13
Steve McCatty-13
Bob McClure-13
Ben McDonald-4
Jack McDowell-11
Sam McDowell-1
Scott McGregor-12
Byron McLaughlin-2
Joey McLaughlin-5
Craig McMurtry-1
Dave McNally-2
Doc Medich-14
Jim Merritt-3
Jose Mesa-9
Gary Mielke-1
Bob Milacki-11
Dyar Miller-3
Alan Mills-3
Craig Minetto-1
Greg Minton-1
Paul Mirabella-2
Angel Miranda-1
Paul Mitchell-8
Dale Mohorcic-4
Sid Monge-3
Larry Monroe-1
John Montague-8
Bill Mooneyham-1
Balor Moore-1
Donnie Moore-1
Mike Moore-16
Carl Moran-1
Angel Moreno-1
Roger Moret-2
Mike Morgan-8
Jack Morris-29
Kevin Morton-3
Jamie Moyer-2
Mike Munoz-4
Rob Murphy-3
Tom Murphy-4
Dale Murray-1
Jeff Musselman-1
Mike Mussina-3
Jeff Mutis-1
Charles Nagy-1
Jaime Navarro-7
Gene Nelson-10
Jeff Newman-1
Rod Nichols-1
Phil Niekro-7
Juan Nieves-1
Al Nipper-8
Dickie Noles-2
Mike Norris-6
Edwin Nunez-5
Jose Nunez-1
Jack O'Connor-4
Blue Moon Odom-3
Bob Ojeda-7
Steve Olin-2
Gregg Olson-4
Steve Ontiveros-1
Jesse Orosco-3
Danny Osborn-1
Claude Osteen-3
Dave Otto-4
Bob Owchinko-1
John Pacella-1
Dave Pagan-1

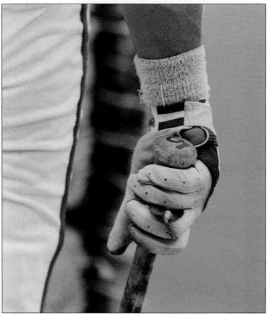

Joe Ledford

Donn Pall-6
Jim Palmer-25
Clay Parker-2
Mike Parrott-8
Larry Pashnick-3
Ken Patterson-3
Roger Pavlik-3
Mike Paxton-6
Orlando Pena-2
Melido Perez-10
Gaylord Perry-17
Jim Perry-2
Stan Perzanowski-2
Adam Peterson-3
Fritz Peterson-2
Mark Petkovsek-1
Dan Petry-20
Skip Pitlock-1
Erik Plantenberg-1
Dan Plesac-4
Eric Plunk-3
Dick Pole-7
Jim Poole-1
Mark Portugal-2
Dennis Powell-3
Ted Power-1
Joe Price-3
Mike Proly-3
Paul Quantrill-2
Scott Radinsky-2
Eric Raich-1
Chuck Rainey-4
Dennis Rasmussen-9
Shane Rawley-11
Jeff Reardon-4
Pete Redfern-7
Jerry Reed-5
Ron Reed-1
Steve Renko-11
Andy Replogle-2
Rick Reuschel-1
Jerry Reuss-9
Bob Reynolds-1
Rick Rhoden-4
Dave Righetti-9
Jose Rijo-6
Allen Ripley-1
Dave Roberts-7
Dewey Robinson-1
Jeff D. Robinson-3
Jeff M. Robinson-4
Ron Robinson-1
Ed Rodriguez-6
Kenny Rogers-4
Ron Romanick-6
Ramon Romero-2
Enrique Romo-4
Steve Rosenberg-2
Gary Ross-6
Dave Rozema-14
Dave Rucker-1
Vern Ruhle-11
Jeff Russell-6
Nolan Ryan-29
Ken Sanders-1
Scott Sanderson-7
Kevin Saucier-1
Rick Sawyer-1
Randy Scarbery-1
Dan Schatzeder-6
Calvin Schiraldi-2
Dave Schmidt-7
Mike Schooler-1
Ken Schrom-4
Ron Schueler-4
Don Schulze-5
Jeff Schwarz-1
Mickey Scott-8
Scott Scudder-4
Rod Scurry-1

Steve Searcy-2
Tom Seaver-7
Diego Segui-1
Jeff Sellers-2
Dave Sells-2
Dick Selma-1
Gary Serum-2
Bob Shirley-3
Wayne Simpson-2
Bill Singer-14
Doug Sisk-1
Jim Slaton-17
Joe Slusarski-1
John Smiley-1
Lee Smith-1
Roy Smith-2
Mike Smithson-21
Nate Snell-4
Lary Sorensen-18
Dan Spillner-3
Ed Sprague-1
Don Stanhouse-2
Bob Stanley-14
Mike T. Stanton-2
Ricky Steirer-2
Dave Stewart-25
Sammy Stewart-10
Dave Stieb-16
Bob Stoddard-1
Tim Stoddard-3
Steve Stone-7
Todd Stottlemyre-14
Les Straker-3
Rick Sutcliffe-1
Don Sutton-8
Bill Swaggerty-1
Russ Swan-3
Bill Swift-11
Greg Swindell-6
Paul Swingle-1
Bob Sykes-1
Frank Tanana-28
Kevin Tapani-4
Scott Taylor-1
Jeff Terpko-2
Walt Terrell-7
Greg Thayer-1
Bobby Thigpen-1
Roy Thomas-1
Stan Thomas-3
Paul Thormodsgard-4
Mark Thurmond-5
Luis Tiant-11
Jay Tibbs-1
Dick Tidrow-6
Dave Tobik-2
Jackson Todd-2
Jim Todd-4
Fred Toliver-1
Pablo Torrealba-2
Mike Torrez-13
Bill Travers-6
Mike Trombley-3
Steve Trout-6
Mike Trujillo-2
John Tudor-7
Jim Umbarger-8
Pat Underwood-1
Tom Underwood-6
Fernando Valenzuela-1
Julio Valera-8
Ed Vande Berg-1
Todd Van Poppel-3
Randy Veres-1
Bob Veselic-2
Frank Viola-14
Pete Vuckovich-5
Tom Waddell-1
Rick Waits-16
Luke Walker-2

Mike Walker-1
Tom Walker-1
Mike Wallace-1
Colby Ward-1
Duane Ward-2
Curt Wardle-2
Mike Warren-3
Gary Wayne-2
Bill Wegman-7
Bob Welch-14
David Wells-7
Chris Welsh-3
Gary Wheelock-3
Ed Whitson-4
Kevin Wickander-1
Bob Wickman-3
Milt Wilcox-14
Bill Wilkinson-1
Al Williams-10
Mitch Williams-2
Mark Williamson-5
Carl Willis-1
Mike Willis-4
Jim Willoughby-1
Frank Wills-5
Jim Winn-2
Rick Wise-9
Bobby Witt-8
Mike Witt-16
Wilbur Wood-4
Dick Woodson-2
Rob Woodward-1
Rich Wortham-2
Clyde Wright-5
Jim Wright-1
Ricky Wright-1
Rich Yett-4
Cliff Young-2
Curt Young-12
Matt Young-12
Geoff Zahn-10

POST-SEASON HITS

Doyle Alexander-4
Joaquin Andujar-2
Jim Beattie-1
Marty Bystrom-1
Bill Campbell-1
Steve Carlton-3
Larry Christenson-1
Jim Clancy-1
Danny Cox-1
Ron Davis-1
Dock Ellis-2
Ed Figueroa-4
Rich Gossage-1
Ron Guidry-4
Tom Henke-1
Roberto Hernandez-1
Ricky Horton-1
Catfish Hunter-6
Grant Jackson-1
Jeff Lahti-1
Rick Langford-1
Aurelio Lopez-1
Sparky Lyle-2
Steve McCatty-1
Tug McGraw-1
Dan Petry-1
Dick Ruthven-2
Dave Stieb-2
Dick Tidrow-1
Mike Torrez-1
John Tudor-4
Bob Walk-1
Milt Wilcox-1

BRETT'S ALL-TIME HOME RUNS

Glenn Abbott-1
Jim Abbott-3
Doyle Alexander-2
Brad Arnsberg-1
Keith Atherton-1
Bob Babcock-2
Howard Bailey-1
Jeff Ballard-1
Scott Bankhead-1
Floyd Bannister-5
Ray Bare-1
Len Barker-2
Steve Barr-1
Francisco Barrios-1
Jose Bautista-1
Dave Beard-1
Juan Berenguer-1
Sean Bergman-2
Tim Birtsas-1
Bert Blyleven-2
Mike Boddicker-2
Mark Bomback-1
Chris Bosio-1
Dennis Boyd-1
Kevin Brown-2
Britt Burns-2
Ray Burris-1
John Butcher-1
Mike Caldwell-1
John Candelaria-2
Chuck Cary-1
John Cerutti-1
Jim Clancy-5
Mark Clark-1
Ken Clay-2
Pat Clements-1
Jim Colborn-1
Steve Comer-2
Keith Creel-1
Danny Darwin-3
Bob Davidson-1
Storm Davis-1
Jose DeLeon-1
Ken Dixon-2
Rich Dotson-2
Dick Drago-3
Rob Dressler-1
Mike Dunne-1
Dennis Eckersley-2
Juan Eichelberger-1
Dave Eiland-1
Roger Erickson-1
John Farrell-2
Alex Fernandez-1
Ed Figueroa-1
Tom Filer-1
Pete Filson-1
Chuck Finley-1
Brian Fisher-1
Mike Flanagan-2
Dave Frost-2
Wayne Garland-1
Jerry Garvin-1
Dave Geisel-1
Dave Goltz-1
Rich Gossage-2
Jim Gott-1
Mike Griffin-1
Ross Grimsley-1
Eddie Guardado-1
Ron Guidry-5
Bill Gullickson-1
Jose Guzman-2
Dave Hamilton-1

Pete Harnisch-1
Paul Hartzell-1
Brad Havens-1
Andy Hawkins-1
Ray Hayward-1
Neal Heaton-1
Tom Henke-1
Jeremy Hernandez-1
Willie Hernandez-1
Roberto Hernandez-1
Ted Higuera-1
Guy Hoffman-1
Darren Holmes-1
Ken Holtzman-2
Burt Hooton-1
Charlie Hough-3
LaMarr Hoyt-1
Jim Hughes-1
Catfish Hunter-1
Roy Lee Jackson-1
Jesse Jefferson-3
Ferguson Jenkins-2
Miguel Jimenez-1
Tommy John-1
Bart Johnson-1
John Henry Johnson-1
Tom Johnson-2
Mike Kekich-1
Jimmy Key-1
Don Kirkwood-1
Bruce Kison-1
Chris Knapp-1
Mark Knudson-1
Tom Kramer-1
Ken Kravec-2
Bill Krueger-1
Pete Ladd-1
Rick Langford-1
Mark Langston-1
Gary Lavelle-1
Jack Lazorko-1
Bill Lee-1
Dave Leiper-1
Mark Leiter-2
Rick Lysander-1
Dennis Martinez-5
Jon Matlack-1
Rudy May-1
Steve McCatty-3
Bob McClure-1
Ben McDonald-2
Jack McDowell-1
Scott McGregor-2
Byron McLaughlin-3
Craig McMurtry-1
Doc Medich-1
Jose Mesa-1
Paul Mitchell-1
Dale Mohorcic-1
Sid Monge-1
John Montague-2
Mike Moore-1
Mike Morgan-1
Jack Morris-5
Jeff Mutis-1
Gene Nelson-5
Mike Norris-1
Edwin Nunez-2
Jim Palmer-2
Mike Parrott-1
Mike Paxton-1
Melido Perez-2
Gaylord Perry-2
Stan Perzanowski-1
Dan Petry-6
Dick Pole-3
Jim Poole-1
Mark Portugal-1
Joe Price-1
Paul Quantrill-1

Dennis Rasmussen-1
Jeff Reardon-1
Pete Redfern-1
Andy Replogle-1
Jerry Reuss-1
Rick Rhoden-2
Dave Righetti-2
Jose Rijo-2
Jeff D. Robinson-1
Jeff M. Robinson-3
Kenny Rogers-1
Ron Romanick-1
Steve Rosenberg-1
Dave Rozema-3
Vern Ruhle-1
Jeff Russell-3
Dan Schatzeder-3
Calvin Schiraldi-1
Dave Schmidt-1
Ron Schueler-1
Jeff Sellers-1
Bob Shirley-1
Bill Singer-1
Mike Smithson-2
Nate Snell-1
Lary Sorensen-2
Dan Spillner-1
Dave Stewart-3
Sammy Stewart-3
Dave Stieb-1
Steve Stone-1
Don Sutton-1
Paul Swingle-1
Frank Tanana-5
Walt Terrell-1
Roy Thomas-1
Mark Thurmond-1
Luis Tiant-2
Jay Tibbs-1
Jim Todd-1
Mike Torrez-3
Bill Travers-2
John Tudor-1
Frank Viola-2
Rick Waits-1
Mike Walker-1
Duane Ward-1
Mike Warren-2
Bob Welch-1
Ed Whitson-1
Milt Wilcox-1
Al Williams-1
Mitch Williams-1
Frank Wills-2
Bobby Witt-1
Curt Young-2
Geoff Zahn-1

POST-SEASON HOME RUNS

Doyle Alexander-3
Ron Davis-1
Rich Gossage-1
Catfish Hunter-3
Grant Jackson-1
Dick Ruthven-1

♦ George Brett and Dave Winfield joke together before a game in 1992. Later that year Brett collected the 3,000th hit of his career. Winfield collected his 3,000th hit during the 1993 season.

Brett on Baseball's All-Time Lists

GAMES
1.	Pete Rose	3,562
2.	Carl Yastrzemski	3,308
3.	Hank Aaron	3,298
4.	Ty Cobb	3,034
5.	Stan Musial	3,026
6.	Willie Mays	2,992
7.	Rusty Staub	2,951
8.	Brooks Robinson	2,896
9.	Robin Yount	2,855
10.	Dave Winfield	2,850
19.	George Brett	2,707

AT-BATS
1.	Pete Rose	14,053
2.	Hank Aaron	12,364
3.	Carl Yastrzemski	11,988
4.	Ty Cobb	11,429
5.	Robin Yount	11,008
11.	George Brett	10,349

RBI
1.	Hank Aaron	2,297
2.	Babe Ruth	2,211
3.	Lou Gehrig	1,990
4.	Ty Cobb	1,961
5.	Stan Musial	1,951
6.	Jimmie Foxx	1,921
7.	Willie Mays	1,903
8.	Mel Ott	1,860
9.	Carl Yastrzemski	1,844
10.	Ted Williams	1,839
22.	George Brett	1,595
	Mike Schmidt	1,595

EXTRA-BASE HITS
1.	Hank Aaron	1,477
2.	Stan Musial	1,377
3.	Babe Ruth	1,356
4.	Willie Mays	1,323
5.	Lou Gehrig	1,190
6.	Frank Robinson	1,186
7.	Carl Yastrzemski	1,157
8.	Ty Cobb	1,139
9.	Tris Speaker	1,133
10.	George Brett	1,119

HITS
1.	Pete Rose	4,256
2.	Ty Cobb	4,191
3.	Hank Aaron	3,771
4.	Stan Musial	3,630
5.	Tris Speaker	3,515
6.	Honus Wagner	3,430
7.	Carl Yastrzemski	3,419
8.	Eddie Collins	3,309
9.	Willie Mays	3,283
10.	Nap Lajoie	3,251
11.	George Brett	3,154
12.	Paul Waner	3,152
13.	Robin Yount	3,142
14.	Rod Carew	3,053
15.	Cap Anson	3,041
16.	Lou Brock	3,023
17.	Dave Winfield	3,014
18.	Al Kaline	3,007
19.	Roberto Clemente	3,000

TOTAL BASES
1.	Hank Aaron	6,856
2.	Stan Musial	6,134
3.	Willie Mays	6,066
4.	Ty Cobb	5,863
5.	Babe Ruth	5,793
18.	George Brett	5,044

HOME RUNS
1.	Hank Aaron	755
2.	Babe Ruth	714
3.	Willie Mays	660
4.	Frank Robinson	586
5.	Harmon Killebrew	573
59.	George Brett	317

DOUBLES
1.	Tris Speaker	793
2.	Pete Rose	746
3.	Stan Musial	725
4.	Ty Cobb	724
5.	George Brett	665

Brett's Career

Regular Season
Yr	G	AB	R	H	2B	3B	HR	RBI	AVG
1973	13	40	2	5	2	0	0	0	.125
1974	133	457	49	129	21	5	2	47	.282
1975	159	634	84	195	35	13	11	89	.308
1976	159	645	94	215	34	14	7	67	.333
1977	139	564	105	176	32	13	22	88	.312
1978	128	510	79	150	45	8	9	62	.294
1979	154	645	119	212	42	20	23	107	.329
1980	117	449	87	175	33	9	24	118	.390
1981	89	347	42	109	27	7	6	43	.314
1982	144	552	101	166	32	9	21	82	.301
1983	123	464	90	144	38	2	25	93	.310
1984	104	377	42	107	21	3	13	69	.284
1985	155	550	108	184	38	5	30	112	.335
1986	124	441	70	128	28	4	16	73	.290
1987	115	427	71	124	18	2	22	78	.290
1988	157	589	90	180	42	3	24	103	.306
1989	124	457	67	129	26	3	12	80	.282
1990	142	544	82	179	45	7	14	87	.329
1991	131	505	77	129	40	2	10	61	.255
1992	152	592	55	169	35	5	7	61	.285
1993	145	560	69	149	31	3	19	75	.266
Totals	2,707	10,349	1,583	3,154	665	137	317	1,595	.305

Division Series
Yr	G	AB	R	H	2B	3B	HR	RBI	AVG
1981	3	12	0	2	0	0	0	0	.167

League Championship Series
Yr	G	AB	R	H	2B	3B	HR	RBI	AVG
1976	5	18	4	8	1	1	1	5	.444
1977	5	20	2	6	0	2	0	2	.300
1978	4	18	7	7	1	1	3	3	.389
1980	3	11	3	3	1	0	2	4	.273
1984	3	13	0	3	0	0	0	0	.231
1985	7	23	6	8	2	0	3	5	.348
Total	27	103	22	35	5	4	9	19	.340

World Series
Yr	G	AB	R	H	2B	3B	HR	RBI	AVG
1980	6	24	3	9	2	1	1	3	.375
1985	7	27	5	10	1	0	0	1	.370
Total	13	51	8	19	3	1	1	4	.373

Joe Ledford